A Biographical Dictionary of
Mull People

MACLEANS

Mainly in the 18th and 19th centuries

Compiled by

Jo Currie

Brown & Whittaker
2002

Published by Brown & Whittaker Publishing, Tobermory, Isle of Mull, PA75 6PR

ACKNOWLEDGEMENTS
Records reproduced by kind permission of Registrar General for Scotland

COVER PHOTOGRAPH: Donald McLean(1807-1877), son of Hugh McLean, Miller of Penmore and Flora Morison, with his wife Mary McLean (1820-1897) daughter of Charles McLean, Boatman in Penmore and Mary McLucas. Donald went on to be miller at Kellan where this picture was probably taken c.1876. After Donald's death, the couple's son Hugh McLean (c.1843-1917) became Miller of Kellan, and a new slated house was built.
Photograph courtesy of their descendant, Mrs Margaret Kinnaird, Nairn.

ISBN 1 904353 00 2

www.brown-whittaker.co.uk

Set in Times New Roman and printed in Fort William, Scotland
by Nevisprint Ltd

Abbreviations, Acknowledgements and Sources

This compilation would not have been possible without the permission and help of authors, publications and institutions scattered through the list of abbreviations below. The abbreviations have been used in the text to indicate to researchers where they might find this information, or further documentation.

AMS/CG	A. Maclean Sinclair *The Clan Gillean*
ARD	Ardnamurchan (Mainland Parish, north east from Mull)
CEN	Censuses of Mull Parishes 1841, 1851, 1861, 1871, 1881
C of S	Church of Scotland
CRB	Civil Registration Births from 1855
CRD	Civil Registration Deaths from 1855
CRM	Civil Registration Marriages from 1855
ERC/Inhabitants	Eric R Cregeen (ed.) Inhabitants of the Argyll Estate, 1779
FASTI	*Fasti Ecclesiae Scoticanae: succession of ministers in the Church of Scotland*
FC	Free Church of Scotland
GK	Gap of Kilninian <u>see</u> FOREWORD
GRO/Scot	General Register Office, Scotland, Edinburgh
GRO/Glouc.	Gloucestershire Record Office
GRV	Gravestone Inscription
ION	Iona quoad sacra parish
JC/MIP	Jo Currie *Mull – the Island and its people*
JPM/HCM	JP Maclean *History of the Clan Maclean*
KLF	Kilfinichen & Kilvicheoun parish
KLN	Kilninian& Kilmore parish
KLS	Kinlochspelve Quoad Sacra Parish
LB	Lochbuy estate
LBP	NAS Lochbuy Papers GD174& GD1
LMD	Lauchlan Maclaine, or his MS diary in GRO/Glouc. Box 8 D3330
LMD/Souls	Lauchlan Maclaine's MS List of Souls in GRO/Glouc.
MPM	Mull Presbytery Minutes NAS CH2/273/2
MRV	Morvern (Mainland area and parish opposite Mull)
NAS	National Archives of Scotland (formerly Scottish Record Office) Edinburgh
NLS	National Library of Scotland, George IV Bridge, Edinburgh
NMB/Inhabitants	Nicholas Maclean Bristol (editor) *Inhabitants of the Inner Isles & C., 1716*
NMB/HD	Nicholas Maclean Bristol *Hebridean Decade*
OPR	Old Parish Register
PG	Pennyghael

PX	Pennycross
QS	Quoad Sacra-parishes introduced 1828 to relieve old parishes
SLN	Salen quoad sacra parish
TBR	Tobermory quoad sacra parish
TRS	Torosay parish sometimes 'Pennygown'
TP	Torloisk Papers in private collection
ULV	Ulva quoad sacra parish

Ag.lab.= agricultural labourer;b.=born; bpt.=baptised or baptism; bro.=brother; b.p.= birthplace; c.=circa; cert.=certified; ch.=child/children; d.=died; dau.=daughter; dec.=deceased; f.=father; GP=general practitioner; gr.-dau.= granddaughter; gr.-s.=grandson; info=information; insp. = inspector; m.=married; min.=minister; mo.=mother; M/S= maiden surname; nat.= natural; nr. = near; q.v.=quod vide= which see; s.=son; unm.=unmarried; us.res.= usual residence; wid.=widow/widower; w.=wife; <=before; >=after;

FOREWORD

This work is a natural follow-up to my previous publication, **Mull Family Names for Ancestor Hunters**, an introduction to the genealogy of Mull families, and an extension of the index to my book **Mull – The Island and its People**, which is a history of events in Mull from 1600-1875 . Readers will appreciate that in the cases of many of the names listed here, it is impossible to find accurate dates of birth, and <, >, and the abbreviation "c." for "circa" are used whenever there is a doubt, or when a median date can be calculated from the various conflicting ages in censuses and death records. Dates without these are usually definite baptism dates. In about 90% of cases, infants were baptised in the first month after their birth.

This book does not claim to be correct. Families specialising in their own genealogy will have had more time to study particular names than I have been able to give to a total of 40,000 families. Because of the many shortcomings in Mull records, this must be regarded as only an approximation to the state of things. And it does not record ALL Macleans in Mull at this time.

Shortcomings in Mull records

Family history enthusiasts should be warned of some of the serious shortcomings in Mull records. There were three parishes in the 18th-19th century, Kilninian & Kilmore (KLN), Torosay (TRS) and Kilfinichen & Kilvicheoun (KLF) also known as 'Ross'. Sometimes the 'parish' of Pennygown was referred to – meaning northern TRS and southern KLN. KLN baptism and marriage records began in 1764, TRS in 1795 (but with no marriages until 1808), KLF in 1804.Only Kilninian people can be traced far back into the earlier 18th century, but this advantage is cancelled out by the non-existence of baptismal and marriage records after c.1827 in the core parish of KLN, when the new quoad sacra parishes of Ulva and Tobermory were being created out of the fringes of Kilninian and Kilmore. There is a story of a fire in the manse of Kilninian burning the records of the period 1827-1855. People born in the Torloisk estates, the Quinish estates, the Mishnish and Mornish estates, and other parts of KLN between 1827 and 1855 can only be re-constructed from censuses. This deplorable loss, or omission, is referred to in this work as the *Gap of Kilninian*, and affects three generations of families.

Another weakness in records is that for 50 years or so before 1828, a Mull Mission looked after the religious needs of a strip of land from Tobermory to below Salen, and the baptismal records have not survived, if they were ever kept. Indeed, wherever there was missionary activity, because a place was remote, the temporary arrangements were responsible for loss of records, or long gaps in continuity. Remote missionary areas like this include Ardmeanach and Burg, Gribun, Glencannel, and townships, now long disappeared, like those on the north shores of Loch na Keill. Salen was also a new parish created to cope with expanded population in the 1820s, and although records exist, they were kept very badly.

Another problem in presenting 'facts' here has been discrepancies in dates. Mull people were notorious for taking years off their ages, and censuses are full of people up to ten years too young, so that census dates in this book do not conform to baptisms and baptisms do not accord with ages at death. But worse still, most Mull people preferred drinking at a funeral to erecting a decent gravestone, and when they did erect a stone it might be 30 or 40 years later, when the dates and ages were forgotten. A surprisingly large number of inscriptions give a date of death several years different from the one in the civil registration. Both in my reading of Maclean correspondence, and in my memories of my own Mull relations, I have noticed what can only be called a mystification of age in operation. Even mature children were not supposed to know the age of their parents. Another unavoidable conclusion is that many Highland people were not very interested in numbers and figures anyway. Their traditions did not include counting, and they seldom referred to dates. Three distinguished Maclean historians, working largely from the same sources, hardly mentioned dates of birth, marriage or death in their accounts of the principal families of the clan. It is amusing also to find in the government enquiries of the 19th century that most of the farmers and crofters had no idea of the extent of land in acres when asked by the commissioners about the amount of land they required. They thought in terms of 'souming' or the number of animals a piece of ground might support.

What alternative sources are there?

Some bonus sources exist, such as the census taken for the Duke of Argyll's estates in 1779, of all the ducal lands in Mull, entitled *Inhabitants of the Argyll Estate, 1779*, edited by the late Eric R. Cregeen and published by the Scottish Record Society, Edinburgh in 1963. It is referred to here as **ERC/Inhabitants**. When using this it is important to know who the landowner was for every place in Mull. It should be stressed that only about 58% of Mull was owned by the duke of Argyll at this time. No other landowner had a private census. A limited number of names appear in some estate rentals of Torloisk and Lochbuy, but these are of tenants only. Tenants were mostly male heads of families, and rentals give no information about wives or children.

The voluminous Lochbuy Papers held by the National Archives of Scotland in Edinburgh (**LBP**) contain correspondence with tenants and other estate dwellers, but no one has indexed the papers for personal names, and one would need to have a very intimate acquaintance with the dramatis personae to be able to tell people apart.

An exceptional source for the most dedicated researchers, is the collection of Maclaine of Scallastle papers in the Gloucestershire Record Office, including **LMD**, the journals of Lauchlan Maclaine. These diaries have many personal references to the people living in Fishnish (then a hugely populated township) Garmony and Scallastle areas of Torosay in the 1820s and 1830s. Again, a great deal of time and patience would have to be expended on going through many haystacks looking for a needle.

Internet links now provide 'clubs' for people with similar family history interests and shared ancestors. Out of the 'Mull List' some spectacular work has come – for example transcripts of diaries, letters and autobiographical writings.

The essential information a researcher must have is the name of the estate his/her relation's house was on, the span of dates of living there, and the name of the land owner of that time – in order to understand the politics of eviction, clearance, or voluntary emigration. It is not enough to know the name of a farm or a parish. Macleans tended to live in marked communities, and were at their densest in the places surrounding a Maclean laird's house. Maclaines were thickest around Moy and Scallastle. Macleans were found almost to the exclusion of other names in Balligown, Tostary, and Burg (around Torloisk) and in Dervaig, Cuin, Druimnacroish, Penmore (around the Macleans of Coll in Quinish).

Spellings of the name Maclean, alternative Christian names and numbers of people with the same name.

The Gaelic proverb, " Like a dog lapping soup the names of the Macleans – Eachunn, Lachunn, Tearlach" (Hector, Lachlan and Charles) has a doleful message for all those who come to family research thinking they will find their Charles Maclean from Mull, only to discover 75 Charles Macleans of roughly the same age. The numbers of similar names are legion. In the census of 1851 alone, there were 305 John Macleans, many of them married to a woman called Mary Maclean. This is due to habits of naming after family members, but the so-called naming patterns must not be taken too seriously. There is a notion abroad that the first son was named after the father's father, the second after the mother's, and similarly with daughters. This is simply not true. It is observed in the breach as often as in the rule. Very often it is the third or fourth son who receives the grandfather's name.

Since most records were entered by a schoolmaster, session clerk, or some such neutral scribe, it was his spelling, and not that of the subject which was used. Maclean can fluctuate between half a dozen spellings in the history of one family. Generally speaking, the spelling Maclaine or McLaine is associated with the Lochbuy estate, and when found in other areas often suggests a refugee from Lochbuy lands. Certain families in the early 19th century insisted on this spelling, but after 1850 gave it up and reverted to McLean, which increasingly became Maclean, as all kinds of pedantic nonsense was written about the correctness of Mc or Mac. Their apostasy reflects the diminishing importance of the family of Lochbuy, or a wish for simplicity. People who emigrated in the 18th century with the name McLane, McLaine or Maclaine do not have to seek Lochbuy explanations. There would then be no significance in the spelling, for even the Maclaines of Lochbuy spelt their name in nine different ways. But those emigrating between 1800 and 1850 with these spellings might have good reason to suppose that they came from Torosay parish and should be wary if they hear a headless horseman galloping by (an intimation that there would be a Lochbuy death).

Every Maclean, regardless of the spelling of the name today, should entertain all possible spellings in the past.

The spelling of Christian names is irrelevant, but alternative names include Sarah=Marion, Hugh=Ewen, Ludovick=Lauchlan, Isabella=Elizabeth=Sibella, Christian=Cirsty, Daniel=Donald, Peter=Patrick. The names now regarded as particularly Highland, such as Fiona, Hamish, Alastair, Iain, Morag, hardly existed in written records in the time we speak of. But people *spoke* the names of Sandy or Alasdair, and the nicknames people actually answered to will be for ever concealed from their descendants.

Macleans did not confine their marriage prospects to other Macleans, so that aliases and alternative forms of surnames absorbed into Maclean families by marriage, such as McLucas=McDougall, Oburn=McDonald, Paterson=McIlphadraig, McShirrie=McKinnon should be studied in **JC/MFN**.

I am grateful to Colin Houston for permission to quote from his grandmother's (Iona McVean) 'Memories of Mull' and to Brian McLean for information in his book, *The Macleans of Killean and Ardfinaig*.

HISTORICAL PREFACE

This biographical dictionary is mainly about Macleans who lived in Mull, Iona and the smaller satellite islands between 1700 and 1900. The clan's genealogy is already well documented by nineteenth century writers like 'A Seneachie', J.P. Maclean and A. Maclean Sinclair, and its exploits are presently being chronicled by a contemporary writer, Nicholas Maclean Bristol. Several other present-day Macleans are also respected scholars in clan matters. One meets many people of the name who have legitimate links with the 'old families' such as the Ardfenaigs, the Lochbuies, the Pennycrosses, the Colls, the Drimnins, the Scallastles, the Uiskens, the Scours, the Torloisks, the Brolasses, and so on. But all Maclean families are equally old, and most of today's Macleans do not have direct *traceable* descent from landed families. Indeed, the territorial titles themselves are not always of great antiquity, and do not necessarily imply that a family *owned* its land. Or again, a territorial title could refer to a brief period of ownership, which entitled that family to use the designation after the land had been sold. This book deals principally with Maclean *followers* – that is with the clansmen and women, the 'kith and kin', the tacksmen, tenants, sub-tenants, cottars and 'connections' of the principal players in the clan story, and not with the chiefs.

Nearly all the far-flung Macleans of today come from families who left Scotland in the 18th and 19th centuries. They left, not only from Mull, but from places all over the West Highlands and Islands, and the Lowlands. But Mull was, in the great days of Duart, the centre and pivot of Maclean life, with ever-widening areas of influence stretching beyond it in concentric circles. Followers of the Clan Gillean took the name as a surname only after surnames had been, as it were, invented. It was only in the 17th century that patronymics gave way to the surnames of McLean, or McDonald, or McDougall. People took the surname of their landowner to accord with the requirement that they should have a surname, and to be known as something more formal than "Fair-haired Hector, son of Big Donald, son of Hector of the Broadsword…" People also changed their surnames with remarkable ease, after they had adopted one name, and found their patrons slipping in the social scale. Thus, in the mid-18th century, nearly everyone in Ulva was a McQuarrie, but after Ulva was bought by McDonalds in 1789, an amazing number of Ulva people became McDonalds. There was nothing disloyal or strange about this. It was practised all over the Highlands as land changed hands, and for less important reasons. What we do not realise today is that in ordinary everyday life there was little need for surnames until about 1750. People might only be required to remember their unnatural surname when offering a rent to a landlord or baptising a child. The rest of the time, a man might just prefer to be known as Big Donald's Hector.

How did this affect Macleans ? With such very large numbers of Maclean followers in Mull, they did not need surnames simply because everyone knew they were Macleans. It was only when they ventured into other territory, or when other clan followers came to live around them, that they needed a surname. If a family of followers of the Torloisk Macleans had remained in Tostary for generations, their nicknames and the place name Tostary served them very well. But when Lachlan Maclean (1720-1799), Laird of Torloisk made up his rent roll, he could not think of anything to call his people but Maclean, and then observed proudly to his visitors that all the men for miles around were Macleans. The concentration of Macleans in his area is greater than anywhere else on Mull.

What was life like for the Macleans in Mull at this time, and what kind of people were they? After their great acquisitions of land in the 15th-16th centuries, the fortunes of the family of Duart took a downward turn, and by the early 17th, the Campbell earls of Argyll had taken over the debts of Duart, and began to demand the interest due to them. Although some payments had been made in the 1650s, the Campbells pursued their debts without reducing interest. The narrative is interrupted here to mention the Battle of Inverkeithing in 1651, which, by its tragic conclusion, wiped out most of the young, able-bodied Macleans from the concentric circles of Maclean domains mentioned earlier. Mull Macleans were decimated, with mainly women and children left to rear cattle and wait for the healing of time. In this interval of weakness the enemy struck. In the 1660s, after the execution of the Marquis of Argyll, the Crown acquired the Mull estates of Duart, telling the new earl of Argyll that it would retain them until Campbell debts to the Crown were paid. But somehow, this arrangement was not carried through, and the ninth earl of Argyll found himself in 1664, infeft in Duart, but with a provisional possession only of the lands of Aros and Brolass. Thus he was able to plant, in other Maclean lands, Campbell tacksmen, but Aros and Brolass kept their Macleans, since the earl did not have absolute power to topple them. This meant that any who remained, after Inverkeithing, of the educated class of Macleans in Torosay, Mornish, Treshnish, Gometra and the coast lands from Oskamull to Gribun were ousted, and either had to leave 'the Country', or stay to become mere tenants or cottars of a clan they hated. It is this situation which was responsible for a widespread belief among scattered Macleans of later times, that they were all related to the chiefs, and had seen better days. Up to a point, this is possibly all too true, yet the people concerned must have been very few in number. But it is significant that, a century later, in the Maclean heartlands, there were no obvious remnants of the gentlemanly class of Macleans. In Brolass, which was now mortgaged rather than disponed, and in Torloisk, which had a separate charter, in Quinish where the Macleans of Coll had right of possession, and in the large estate of Lochbuy, which spread out on both sides of Duart, there were still families of status to give leadership to Maclean followers. But they didn't all oppose the Campbells.

We now enter upon a turbulent period when deputies, or tutors, mainly of the family of Brolass, acted as spokesmen for the Maclean of Duart interest in what might be called 'negotiations' with the Argylls. But these gentlemen seemed to do little for their clan's advantage. The Campbells issued decreets of removing to eleven respected Macleans in 1673, and two years later sent letters of caption to hundreds of individual Mull Macleans, gentles and commoners alike. The names of these

Macleans can be found in *Highland Papers*, vol. 1 edited by J.R.N. MacPhail for the Scottish History Society, Edinburgh 1914. They were all designated 'rebells', for having been ordered to 'flitt and remove themselves, their wifes, bairns, families, servants, sub-tenants, cottars, goods, gear ...' and not having done so.Required to attend a criminal trial at Inveraray, they understandably declined to do so. They were on the run. This was the second exodus of Macleans from Mull, and judging by the number of names, it was very large. The diaspora was probably contained within Gaelic-speaking Scotland, but outwith the jurisdiction of the Campbells of Argyll, and this explains the intensification of Maclean population in outer bands of the aforesaid concentric circles. It was a wonder that there were any Macleans left in Mull at all.

When the twenty-two-year-old Maclean chief, Sir John of Duart, finally crawled out of his bolt hole at Cairnburgh in 1692 to go into exile abroad, he left behind him possibly several hundred clansmen who had escaped letters of caption, and who certainly did not know about, or believe in, the legal justification the Argylls gave for their actions. Maclean 'propaganda', in the form of a passionate outpouring of Gaelic poetry about the noble deeds of the clan naturally never mentioned that they had lived above their income, refused to pay feu duties to the Campbells or otherwise neglected business. Draconian methods employed by the Campbells were gradually relaxed, although they allowed themselves certain pleasurable reprisals, as they had done with the McDonalds in Glencoe in the same year of 1692. In the rest of the 1690s, famine added a brake to the regeneration of Mull Macleans.

With such constant stops and starts, the core of the clan was now to be found outside the Maclean heartland of Mull, and in the early 18th century began to find its way overseas. The 1715 and 1745 Jacobite uprisings added a different breed of Maclean to the outgoing trickle, but the muster roll of Prince Charles Edward Stuart's army, now published as *No Quarter Given*, clearly shows that relatively few Macleans took part in the Battle of Culloden in 1746. This was due to the arrest of the Chief, Sir Hector Maclean, in Edinburgh in June 1745, and to the presence of Campbells (who were on the Government side) in Mull. Drimnin and Ardgour Macleans, however, were in the forefront. Some were transported as criminals to the American colonies for having taken part in the 1715 rebellion. Many Macleans in the mid-18th century went to Jamaica, where they were successful in commerce and in the professions. American Macleans now appeared with strange spellings of the name, and possibly with different names altogether. Meanwhile the remnant in Mull, having seen the suffering derived from rebellion, compromised with Campbell tacksmen, volunteered for the military in the service of the king, in the Seven Years War, and later found themselves fighting against their own clansmen in the American Revolutionary War.With the exception of the families of Brolass, Coll, Torloisk, Lochbuy, Scallastle, Calgary, and some of the so-called 'half-gentry', their relations, in Ardfenaig, Scour, Uisken, Ardchrishnish, Rossall and Kilbrenan, the early 19th century Macleans in Mull came from humble and obscure farming stock. Macleans who had remained in the Highlands beyond the reach of Campbell jurisdictions were now scattered into the Lowlands and England as well, and the ruined Duart Castle was for them a fitting symbol of past glories. The Macleans in this collection of biographical sketches are therefore, by definition, and by the fact that they were still in Mull after all the convulsions detailed above, the Remnant of Mull Macleans. The Macleans who had left earlier were more likely to be ancestors of present-day Macleans who know that their families have spent two hundred years elsewhere. Yet the Remnant depicted here were themselves to be the antecedents of a new wave of exiles, who in turn were to generate another diaspora. In the clearances of the 1840s-1860s, two thirds of the Macleans in this book, with their dependants, were to leave for other parts of Scotland, and for England, Canada, Australia and New Zealand.

THE CHIEFS OF THE 18th and 19th CENTURIES

Maclean, Sir John (1670-1716) 20th chief of Maclean and 4th baronet of Morvern, was s. of Sir Allan Maclean, 19th chief & Julian Macleod. His f. d. young, and Sir Hector succeeded at the age of 4. He was looked after by guardians – Lachlan Maclean of Brolass and Lachlan Maclean of Torloisk, who negotiated with the earl of Argyll about repayment of supposed Maclean debt to Campbells. When the 2 guardians d. in 1686 and 1687, Sir John became responsible for his own affairs, and at the age of 18 was in the Battle of Killiecrankie. When he returned to Mull it was to hide out in the island fortress of Cairnburgh, as the Campbells of Argyll had taken over Duart. He left in 1692, advising his Mull followers to make the best of the Campbell take-over. He lived in France, where he m. Mary McPherson. There were 5 daus. and one s. – Hector – b. Calais 1703. He returned to Scotland after the death of Queen Anne, took part in the Battle of Sheriffmuir, and d. at Gordon Castle in 1716.

Maclean, Sir Hector (1703-1750) 21st Chief of Maclean, s. of Sir John Maclean & Mary McPherson, he was b. Calais when his parents were *en route* for London where they were to be received by the new queen, Anne, who was offering an indemnity to Jacobites. Sir John's failure to appear made his situation ambivalent, but the Macleans continued to support the exiled "James III" – the 'Chevalier'. In c.1707 Hector was placed with the Macleans of Coll, spending his formative years with them in Coll and Quinish until 1721, when he studied at Edinburgh and Paris. He visited his family in 1725, returned to France, remaining there until his fatal attempt to take part in the Rising of 1745, when he was arrested in Edinburgh on suspicion of making plans for a rebellion. He was released after Culloden, and d. in Rome in 1750.

Maclean, Sir Allan (1710-1783)22nd Chief of the clan Maclean and 6th baronet of Morvern 1750-1783, he was of the Brolass Macleans, but their lands, mostly around L. Scridain, and those areas preceding the Ross of Mull, were mortgaged to the Duke of Argyll, who received the rents, and allowed Sir Allan's family to live at Inchkenneth. He succeeded his 3rd cousin, Sir Hector Maclean, a Jacobite sympathiser. He had a formidable mo., Isabel Maclean of Ardgour, 'Lady Brolass', still alive in 1759, when she was one of the witnesses in the LB incarceration case. He m. 1750 **Una Maclean**, dau. of Hector **Maclean** of Coll, 'Young Lady Brolass', and by her had 3 surviving daus., Maria, Sibella, Anne. A boy, the wished-for heir, d.c.1755. Young Lady Brolass d.1760. Sir Allan was a courteous, if inwardly agitated, host to Johnson and Boswell on their tour of the Hebrides in 1773. He had been persuaded to go to law with the 5th Duke of Argyll to regain all the Duart lands, but the case was successful only in Brolass, which was restored to him. Sir Allan seems to have had some nat. ch., but only the name of one comes down to us – Malcolm Maclean (q.v.), fl. 1780s-1840s.

Maclean, Sir Hector (c.1762-1818) 23rd Chief,was commissioned Ensign in the 2nd battalion of the 84th Regiment in N. America in 1775, when he was only 13. He succeeded Sir Allan Maclean (q.v.) in 1783 as 23rd Chief of the Clan Maclean at the age of 21. He was bro.-in-law of Allan Maclean (q.v.) of Torloisk and of the Royal Highland Emigrants, in which Hector served under John Small, but was sent home shortly after the Siege of Savannah owing to ill health. He then lived with his sister Janet (q.v.) in London, and is believed to have stayed in London for the rest of the war. It is significant that when applying for promotion for his young bro.-in-law, Allan Maclean represented Hector as next in line for the Chiefship of Maclean, and said a commission would confer favour on the whole clan. Little else is known of the life of this Chief, who remained unm., and 'lived a retired life during the greatest portion of his days.'

Maclean, Sir Fitzroy Jeffreys Grafton (c.1770-1847) 24th of Duart, 8th baronet of Morvern; half-bro. of Sir Hector, he was s. of Daniel Maclean & Margaret Wall, called after the duke of Grafton, Prime Minister 1767-70. He came into the title in 1818. He had idea of buying back lands of Duart, held by the Campbells since the 17th C., but at the time of Fitzroy's accession to the title, were on the market. His moment passed him by. Duart, its castle now a complete ruin, had been purchased by Charles Macquarie, who sold it again in 6 years' time, there being again no intervention from Sir Fitzroy, who was affectionately dismissed by Lachlan Macquarie, governor of NSW as a 'great jaw'. Sir Fitzroy had m. 1794 Elizabeth Kidd, and was 1st chief of Maclean since Sir John to have a direct heir in the male line (and a son to spare). Several other ch. d. young. He lived mainly in England, and although reported to be planning to visit Mull, no record appears to exist of such a visit.

Maclean, Sir Charles Fitzroy (1798-1883) 25th of Duart,9th baronet of Morvern, s. of Sir Fitzroy & Elizabeth Kidd, he had a very English education at Eton and Sandhurst, and m. in 1831 Emily Marsham, dau. of a canon of Windsor. There were 4 daus., and an heir, Fitzroy Donald Maclean. Sir Charles lived in Gibraltar and at Folkestone, England, where he d. in 1883.

Maclean, Sir Fitzroy Donald (1835-1936) continued the army tradition of his family, serving in the Crimea, and at the battle of Alma and siege of Sebastapol. A dedicated traveller, he included Scotland in his many journeys. After m. 1872 an Englishwoman, Constance Marianne Holland Ackers, the couple expressed a desire to return to Maclean roots in Mull, and when he was over 70 Sir Fitzroy concluded a deal with the owners of the Duart estate to buy back the ruined castle and restore it. This was done, and the castle, without the estate, was formally opened in 1912. Sir Fitzroy's ch. were Hector Fitzroy, 1873; Charles Lachlan, 1874; Fitzroy Holland, 1876 (d.1881); John Marsham, 1879 and Finvola Marianne, 1887.

THE NAMES

McLean, Abraham (1773) an Abraham McLean was bpt. 21 Feb. 1773, nat. s. of John McLean & Mary McQuarie in Mingary, but it is not clear that this is the same Abraham who later m. **Catherine McKay** and had Alexander (1794-1860) & Gillean who was bpt. in Tobermory 1803. **KLN OPR**

McLean, Abraham (1819) another Abraham McLean was bpt. 30 Jan. 1819, s. of John McLean (q.v. <1795) & Sarah Livingston in TBR **KLN OPR**. He was not in **CEN TBR 1851** at Breast with his family, when his f. was shoemaker aged 68, his mo. 61.

Maclaine, Adam Cameron (c.1816) *2nd s. of Lachlan Maclaine, s. of Allan, s. of Lachlan, s. of Allan. bro. to Hector Maclaine* of Lochbuy. So described on his copy of the LB entail. **GRO/Glouc**. Lived in Paisley. His mo. was Mary Cameron dau. of Duncan Cameron. He was involved in the 'Shoemaker's Claim' to Lochbuy, but d. < his bro. Allan Maclaine (q.v.- 1814-1881).

Maclaine, Alexander (<1710->1788) 'Sanders' tacksman of Callachilly, he was an old man in 1788 when he wrote to warn Murdoch of LB about Gillean Maclaine's fraud and artifice over the ownership of kelp shores. *"... he erazed my excepted shoar of Callachilly from the principal tack"* **GD174/1411/1** Sanders Maclaine seems to have been a relative of LB, popular with correspondents who sent compliments to him. He may have been f. of Drs Donald & Andrew Maclaine, as there is some evidence of his son Hugh being the same man as the Tobermory wine mercht. If this was so, his relations with Hugh were strained in 1788 when Sanders spoke of *"many innumerable insults passed on me as a ffather by a son who...wants to bring the ffather to a narrow corner ..."* **NAS GD 174/1411/2**. Sanders' w. was still alive in 1788, but remains unidentified.

McLean, Rev. Alexander (1721-1765) s. of the min. of KLN and poet, John McLean, & Isabel, dau. of Charles McNeill Ban. He was assistant and successor to his f., and m. 1750 **Christian** (d. 1781) dau. of Donald **Maclean** of Torloisk. Their s. John was b. 1752, drowned c.1780 at Halifax Nova Scotia; Lachlan (b.1754) became military governor of Nova Scotia. It is not confirmed that Isabel his dau. ever m. She was companion to Mrs Maclean of Torloisk in 1780. Mary (q.v.) b. 1757 m. 1778 the lawyer John Campbell, 2nd s. of Dr Robert Campbell of Smiddy Green in Fife who d. 1821. They are known to have had s. Robert Campbell in 1779. A letter from Mary is in **NAS GD174/1334**. LMD visited her in London in 1815. **GRO LMD**. Of another s. Donald nothing is known. Alexander Maclean was ill for many years from a debilitating disease which prevented him from travelling in his parish, and presbytery meetings were held at his house to facilitate his participation. **MPM**

McLean, Dr Alexander (1725-1786 or 1800) 1st of Pennycross was s. of Charles of Killunaig & Marion McLean, sister of Donald of Torloisk (q.v.), but several conflicting b. & d. dates have been published. From sasines, it would appear that he d. 1786, when land transfers were made to his s., or 1800. His relationship with the Torloisk family by his mo. bonded these 2 families for generations. He m. 1760 **Una McGillivray** of Pennyghael, with 2 known ch. – Archibald (q.v. 1761-1830) & Catherine, of whom little has come down, except that she m. a Major Donald McLean of the Royal Scots. Una cooked 'a very good dinner' for Johnson & Boswell in 1773, and Dr McLean was *"one of the stoutest and most hearty men I have seen – more of the farmer than of the doctor."* Dr Alexander pronounced Mr Johnson*"a hogshead of sense"*.

McLean, Alexander (c.1754-1835) 'Alasdair Ruadh', of Coll, 2nd s. of Hugh McLean of Coll & Janet Macleod of Talisker, and younger bro. of Donald, 'Young Col', the guide of Johnson & Boswell in the Hebrides, who was drowned in 1774. He abandoned study of law at his bro.'s death, and was served heir to his f. Hugh, in 1790, when he was described as Capt. Alexander Maclean of Coll. He m. **Catherine Cameron**, eldest dau. of Capt. Allan Cameron of Glendessary, by whom he had one s. and 6 daus. – Hugh, Janet, Sibella, Catherine, Maria, Marion and Breadalbane. In 1818 he was laird of Coll, Quinish in Mull, Rum and Muck. He lived latterly at Quinish, KLN, and d. 10 Apr. 1835. **JPM/HCM JC/MIP NMB/HD**

McLean, Alexander (c.1770) was m. to **Isabel**

('Bell') **McLean** before 1799, and they lived in Crogan for most of their lives, having 9 ch. bpt. in **TRS OPR** – Alexander 1799, Allan 1800, Hector 1803, Janet 1805, Donald 1805, Marion 1811, Cirsty 1812, Robert 1814, Jean 1816. Some of those ch. remained in TRS parish, where their names are spelt 'McLaine'. **TRS OPR**

McLean, Lt.-Col. Alexander (1777-1859) of Uisken, s. of Duncan McLean & Mary McLaine, he remains one of the most controversial of McLean personalities. Unm., he retired to Millport on the island of Great Cumbrae where he passed his days planning and altering the destination of his fortune. When his Will was made public, it was challenged by relations, who failed in their claim, whereupon the money was applied to the education of Maclean boys, so long as they did not spell their names 'Maclaine'. **JC/MIP GRO Testament of Alexander Maclean**

McLean, Alexander (<1780) was 'of the Sloop *Dick of Greenock*' on 11 Apr. 1801 when he m. **Janet McLean** in Ensay KLN. A first s., Hugh, is not in **KLN OPR**, but Hector 1897, Mary Ann 1808, Isabel 1812, Helen 1814 and Alexander 1816 were bpt. at Balligown, KLN, and it is not clear that the family at Ledag in **CEN KLN 1841**, when Alexander is a carpenter, are the same, although an Isabella and a Helen 20 might suggest this. But another Helen McLean aged 20 at Portmore casts doubts again.

McLaine, Alexander (<1780) lived in Saorphein KLF with his w. **Flora McGilvray** < beginning of extant **KLF OPR**, in which only the bpt. of Hugh 1805, John 1807, Hugh 1808, Allan 1810, and another unnamed ch. in 1812 are recorded. A man of this name is in Whyte's *Dictionary of Scottish Emigrants to Canada* as leaving. c.1813, but is unlikely to be him. His s. Hugh was a well-known mercht. in Iona, and d. at Martyr's Bay, Iona, 4 Nov. 1863 aged 55.

McLean, Alexander (<1780) Two Alexander McLeans who m. **Christina McLean**s make a problem of identification. Both m. in 1803, one at Langamull, one in Mingary KLN. Between them they had 13 births: Janet 1803, Janet 1805, Mary 1807, Archibald 1808, Hugh 1808, Hector 1810, Donald 1810, Flora 1812, Flora 1814, Donald 1816, Christina 1823 and twins Lachlan & William 1825.

McLean, Alexander (c.1780) m. **Mary Buchanan** in Sorn, KLN <1812 and had Ann 1812, Chirsty 1814, Catherine 1815, Flora 1817.

Mary poss. dau. bpt. 1784 of Donald Buchanan, Peinalbanach & Mary McLachlan.

McLean, Alexander (c.1784-1821) youngest s. of John McLean of Langamull, he was a med. stud. at Edin. Univ. in Gregory Class list 1803-1805. He was considered by Earl of Selkirk in 1813, in his plan for Red River Settlement, who had *"no information as to this young doctor's character and qualifications"*. He d. unm. at Cuttack, East Indies 29 Sep.1821.

McLean, Alexander (c.1785-1873) s. of Allan McLean & Mary McMillan, he m. **Flory McInnes**, and lived in Ensay & Kilmory, KLN, in 1820s when Marjory, Lachlan & Margaret were bpt. **CEN KLN 1851** reveals he was b. Ardgour, but his w. was a Mull girl. Lachlan became a Sheriff Clerk Depute at Tobermory, while living at home in McKenzie Street, TBR. Alexander & Flora were still in TBR in 1861, when he was a feuar of 72 (b. Kilmallie). By 1871 he had been blind for 3 years and now a wid., 85, lived with his dau. Margaret Wilson, also widowed, and his gr.-ch., May Wilson 17, Flora Wilson 14, Margaret Jane Wilson 12, Lachlan Wilson 8, all 'scholars' b. TBR. **CEN KLN/TBR 1851, 1861, 1871**.

Maclean, Alexander (1791-1876) "Sandy Pennycross" s. of Archibald Maclean (q.v.) of PX & Alice Maclean of Torranbeg, educated at Glasg. Univ.; succeeded his f. in PX title 1830. He was exactly of an age with 'young' Murdoch Maclaine of LB, with whom he had land arrangements, and letters about him are in **NAS GD174**. Donald Maclean WS was perplexed by his daus. teasing each other about him: *"I see Chirsty constantly joking Mary in her letters about Sandy Pennycross – I would greatly prefer seeing her going to her grave than form such a connection, and that fully as much on Sandy's account as hers … I know that Sandy would rather drown himself …"* Financial troubles with PX estate caused Sandy to sell parts. *"Sandy is so occupied adorning Pennyghael that it will prove his ruin – furnishing it without the means of doing so…"* PG was sold to Mr Auldjo in 1829, and in 1840 Sandy m. **Charlotte Brodie Maclean**, Kintyre, 1840 – 2 sons, Archibald John (q.v.) 4th of PX & Allan Thomas Lockhart; 3 daus. Alice, Charlotte, Mary. Lived at PX & Carsaig, being one of very few resident lairds in Mull in troubled mid-19th C., and one who was unwilling to evict. **JC/MIP. AMS/CG**

McLean, Alexander (1802) bpt. 7 Nov. 1802) s. of John McLean (q.v.) schoolmaster, Balligown &

Margaret McCallum. His parents were m. publicly 26 Jan. 1802. He and his bro.were reported to have behaved badly at a funeral in 1836. **JC/MIP p.183**.

McLean, Alexander (c.1805-c.1849) ploughman at Assapol, KLF, he m. **Cirsty McEachern**, Ardtun, KLF, 8 Aug. 1832. Marion was bpt. 1833, Hector 1846. Other ch. were Donald c.1835,Ann (Agnes) c.1839, Angus c.1848. His w. was a wid. in **CEN KLF 1851**.

McLean, Alexander (c.1809) b. MRV but lived KLF. In Jan. 1836 he m. **Isabella McPherson**, TBR. In **CEN KLF 1851** at Kinlochscridain he was a mason, 42, with Isabella 34, Hugh 14, Mary 12, Allan 10, Duncan 8, Margaret 6, John 4, Donald 6 mo.

McLean, Alexander (c.1815) went to parish of Dunlop, Ayrshire, returning to Mull Dec. 1842 to m. **Christian McPhail** (bpt. 14 July 1814) dau. of Duncan McPhail & Flora McKinnon in Garmony TRS. He became an employee of John Campbell, 'Factor Mor' at Ardfenaig in the 1840s, but emig. to Moreton Bay, Australia on the Marmion from Liverpool 28 Aug. 1852 with his w.'s McPhail relations. The Emig. Soc. commented that he had too many young ch. (3 girls, Jessy, Ketty and Effy). His dau. Euphemia McLean (q.v.) gave evidence at the inquest at Mt. Gambier into the suicide of her aunt, Sarah McPhail or Macdonald, w. of John Macdonald from Iona, in 1868.

McLean, Alexander (b.1817) s. of John McLean (q.v.) miller in Penmore, KLN & Catherine McKinnon. He was in **CEN KLN 1851** as boatman aged 33, unm.

McLean, Alexander (c.1822) m. a **Mary**, and in **CEN KLF 1861** of Killunaig he was 38 and a mason, with Mary 39, Jane 15, John 13, Neil 11 ('scholars'), Margaret 9, Allan 7, Mary 5, & Catherine 6 mo. – living in 1 room.Absence of bpts. for this family suggests FC or Baptist affiliations. 5 of these ch. were still with their parents at Kinloch, KLF in 1871.

McLean, Alexander (c.1823) b. Kilbride, Isle of Coll he was a shoemaker 32 in Penmore when his s. Neil was b. 10 Nov. 1855. He m. in Glasgow in 1852 Catherine McLucas from Penmore who was 29 in 1855.

McLean, Alexander (1825-1904) bpt. 31 May 1825, s. of John McLean, tenant, Suie, KLF & his w. Isabella Cameron, Knocknafenaig, who had m. 25 Mar. 1825. Port Elgin Cemetery, Sanctuary Park, Pt. Lot 11, Con 9 Saugeen Township, Ontario has an inscription "*In memory of Alexander Maclean, died January 29 1904 aged 79 years. A native of the Ross of Mull. In memory of Elizabeth McLean* [his sister, bpt. 12 Oct.1820] *born 2 October 1820, died August 18th 1899, a native of the Ross of Mull.*" His mo. Isabella Cameron, also d. in Canada in 1879 aged 88.

McLean, Alexander (c.1884-1945) police sergeant, m. to **Flora Nicolson**, he d. in W. Highland Cottage Hospital, Oban, 1945, his us. res. Thornliebank, Tobermory. His f. was Alexander McLean, crofter, his mo. Marion McPhee.

Maclean, Alice (c.1719–1755) dau. of Donald Maclean of Torloisk (q.v.); a poet of merit; she was tricked into marr. c.1739 by **Lachlan McQuarrie** of Ulva, who wrote her a letter purporting to be from her sweetheart saying he was marrying another. She m. McQuarrie with a tocher (dowry) of 1,500 merks. She had 8 ch. and d. aged about 35. Reputed to be the author of several versions of a song always on the theme of her own sorrow: "*From ye man that I love tho' my heart I disguise/I wou'd freely distinguish the wretch I despise.*" That she was still alive in 1751 is shown by a letter from her bro. to her husb.: "*I am impatient to know what comes of Poor Alice.*" **JPM/HCM; AMS/CG; JC/MIP**

Maclean, Alicia (<1769) a marriage in Edinburgh 23 Mar. 1785 of David Brown surgeon in the General Hospital Tron Parish & *Miss Allicia, High Kirk Parish daughter of deceased McLean of Torloisk Isle of Mull* may refer to the nat. dau. of Hector Maclean (q.v.) of Torloisk, as the only other dec. Maclean of Torloisk could not have had a dau. of marr. age. Descendants of David Brown should be alerted to this possibility of a blot, or a rose, on their escutcheon, depending on their viewpoint.

MacLaine, Alicia (1774-1834) dau. of Gillean Maclaine of Scallastle (q.v.) & Marie McQuarrie, dau. of Lachlan McQuarrie of Ulva, she was called after her gr.-mo. Alice Maclean (q.v.) of Torloisk. She m. 22 Apr. 1793 **John Wood**, solicitor, Edinburgh, some of their ch. John, an ensign, Flora, James and Gillean Maclaine Wood being mentioned in **GRO/Glouc**. and in **LMD**.

McLean, Allan (1724-1792) of Drimnin MRV. Not strictly a Mull Maclean, he was proprietor of Killean, TRS for a short time, and his s. Charles, who m. Maria, dau. of Sir Allan Maclean (q.v.) of

Duart, was proprietor of Broloss just as briefly. He had 2 wives, **Ann Maclean** of Broloss (sister of Sir Allan), then Mary or **Mally Maclaine** (q.v.) of Lochbuy (1740-1831). His s. Donald Maclean WS (q.v.) was an important character in Mull's history. **JC/MIP**

Maclaine,Allan (<1750) s. of Lachlan Maclaine of the earlier Scallastle Maclaines, who served in the army and was reputedly killed in America in the 7 Years War. Allan was raised in Scallastle, but left for Greenock 1774. See Maclaine, Allan (1814-1881) his gr.s. of the 'shoemaker's claim'.

McLean, Allan (c.1750-1838) from **GRV** at Keil, Morvern: *"In memory of Allan McLean, late tenant of Kilmory, Mull, who died at Blaich, Ardgour February 4th 1838 aged 88 years, and of Mary McMillan his wife who died July 18th 1841 aged 80 years. And of their son Charles, for many years of the Inland Revenue, who died at Cuil, Duror, Appin, August 1st 1863 aged 78 years. Also of Hannah their daughter who died at Cuil, Duror, November 17 1871 aged 75 years."*

McLean, Dr Allan (1759-1827) *'the red-haired doctor with the warm eyes'*, s. of Dr John Maclean (1724-1808) & Christina Maclean (d.1808) in Brolass, he was the subject of various praise poems in Gaelic. In 1800 he was lieut. surgeon in the 4th Fencible Infantry, and served with Cameron Highlanders as a surgeon. On leaving the army he settled in Brolass, and m. at the age of 54, Miss **Flora Maclaine** (q.v.) dau. of Murdoch Maclaine (q.v.) of Lochbuy, who was 17. Between 1814 and 1826 9 ch. were b. to the couple, who lived at Rossal, then part of LB estate. Domhnall Ban Mac Gilleain d. in 1827, and his w. 'Flory Lochbuy' left Mull to give her ch. a good education at Ayr. She met and m. a medical friend of her husb.'s also widowed, Dr William Whiteside. For the ch. of Allan and Flory see her entry. **JC/MIP; AMS/CG**

McLean, Allan (1760-1853) 'Ailean Sgoilear' schoolmaster in Iona, s. of John Maclean, Acharn, and uncle to the Rev. Neil Maclean (q.v.), tutor to the ch. of Charles Macquarie and later min. of Ulva Parish, who received his extensive primary education in Iona from his uncle.He was superannuated, a wid. aged 90 in **CEN ION 1851**, but the name of his w. does not appear in records.

McLean, Allan (<1760) living in Gometra when he m. **Mairon McDonald** 3 Feb.1784, the couple remained there for at least 15 years, and their ch. James 1785, Ann 1789, Marion 1791, Donald 1793, Lauchlan 1795, Mary 1799 were bpt. on this island. In 1801, another Lauchlan was bpt. at Fanmore KLN.

McLean, Allan (<1760) in Lagganulva at time of his marr. to **Flora McDougall**, 19 Jun. 1792, he and his w. lived on Braes of Lagganulva until they moved to Fanmore in early 1800s. Bpts in **KLN OPR**: Catherine 1793, John 1795, Hector 1800, Hugh (q.v.) 1802, Flora 1805. Hector was to emig. to Australia with his w. Flora McKinnon & prob. other siblings, Hugh hanging on in Fanmore through 1841 & 1851 censuses, but eventually leaving with his w. Sarah & ch. whose bpts. are missing in GK.

Maclaine, Allan (1772-1843) s. and heir of Gillean McLaine (q.v.) of Scallastle, he was first trained for the law, but gave this up in 1791. He has more documentation than most Mull men, letters to and about him being in **NAS GD174, NAS GD 1/1003, GRO**. He m. **Marjory Gregorson**, dau. of Angus G. of Ardtornish in 1797, his sons Gillean (q.v.) and Angus (q.v.) being b. in 1797 and 1799. As Heir of Entail to the LB estate, he opposed all of Murdoch Maclaine's plans to sell off marginal lands to pay estate debts, and refused to answer letters from lawyers and creditors. He removed his infant s. Angus from his mo., accused Dr Donald Maclaine (q.v.) of cuckolding him, these and other acts causing him to be certified insane in 1807, and ordered to pay for the aliment of his w., who, with her Gregorson relations brought up his 2 sons. He was confined in Gordon Castle, nr. Musselburgh, where his 'keeper' did not dare to control him, and where his bro. Archibald pronounced him mad.

McLean, Allan (c.1785-1857) s. of Hugh McLean & Marion McLean (M/S McLean) he d. aged 71 at Catchean, Ross of Mull 10 Feb. 1857. His w. was **Mary McLean** (q.v.) (c.1790-1882), dau. of Lachlan Ban Maclean (q.v.) Innkeeper, Bunessan. The marr. had taken place on 18 Apr. 1825, when Allan was from Van Diemen's Land (Tasmania), although b. Kilfinichen, and Mary, from Bunessan,must have been about 35. There were no ch. of the marr. recorded in Mull OPRs. In **CEN KLF 1851** the couple are in Squet-lolla, nr. Creich, when Allan is 65 and Mary 60. The presence of a visitor, Allan McCallum, underlines Mary's relationship with the McCallum family in Tobermory, her sister Catherine's ch. She was the aunt of the outspoken and controversial lawyer John McCallum.

McLean, Allan (c.1790-1874) farmer, s. of Angus McLean and Flora McLean, he m. **Euphemia McLean** prob. c.1834. Because of GK, no marr. or bpts. in KLN OPR. But from censuses at Fanmore, the ch. were Angus c.1834, Mary c.1836, John c.1839, Flory c.1841, Allan c. 1843 & Donald c.1846. Allan d. 1 Jan.1874 at Fanmore KLN aged 85, of infirmities of old age, being ill for only 3 wks. John McLean, his s. gave info. in **CRD**. Donald was a letter carrier (postman) in 1861. In 1871 still at Fanmore, Allan is 82, Euphemia 64, John unm. 30, Flora unm. 26 . Euphemia d. Fanmore 1875, aged 67. Their s. John McLean d. Fanmore 1905 aged 65.

McLean, Allan (1795-1855) d. at Croig Inn KLN 13 Dec.1855 aged 57. Had been m. to (1) **Mary McLean** (2) **Margaret McNeill**. His f. was Lachlan McLean (q.v.), his mo. Mary McFadyen, his 2nd w. being present at his death. Allan McLean when first m. to Mary McLean 8 Mar. 1824, was from Inivea and Mary from Arin. They had Mary 1825 and Anne 1826 bpt at Inivea. The next ch. are in GK. In 1841 at Penmore Allan McLean is 40, Mary 34, Ann 14, Cate 12, Marry 10, Jessie 8, Flora 6, Lauchlan 4, & Ellen 6 mo. Mary must have d. shortly afterwards, as Peggy is the 46-year-old w. in 1851 census at Penmore, with her stepson Allan 9, and others,and her own ch. Flora aged 1. Peggy McNeill d. a pauper in Argyll Terrace, TBR in 1863 aged 52, wid. of Allan McLean Penmore. Her f. was Lachlan McNeill, her mo. Flora McKinnon, and her death was cert. by Archibald McNeill, shoemaker in Ledag. **KLN OPR; KLN CRD; CEN KLN 1841**

McLean, Allan (<1800) a man who has had to be reconstructed from his wid.'s details, he m. **Euphemia McKinnon** <1833 and d. <1841, leaving her to make a living as a stocking knitter, with 1 dau. Mary b. c.1833 & John b. c.1835. Effy is in Salen in 1841 with John 5, in Salen 1851 aged 55 with Mary 17, John 15, and in Salen 1861 with John 25. She d. at Salen 17 Jan. 1864 aged 70, of paraplegia. Her parents were John McKinnon & Catherine McPhail, and info was supplied by the faithful John.

McLean, Allan (c.1804-1873) ferryman at Portonan, (Port Donan) TRS m. to **Jean Campbell** 22 Mar. 1827 in TRS OPR. In **CEN. TRS 1861** he was b. KLF, but 1851 census says TRS. In **CEN. TRS 1871** he was in Crogan Village, wid. 58, wool weaver (no bp.) with s. John marr. 29, seaman, Mary dau. (in law?) marr.

27, Allan (John's) s., and with Donald McArthur, gr.s. aged 3, all b. KLS. In 1881 Allan is gone, John is head aged 39, seaman, Mary, John's w. 37, Mary his dau. 9, Colin his s. 6, Jessie the youngest,2 mo.

McLean, Allan (b. c.1807) MRV but m. to a KLN woman and with 5 of his ch. b. KLN, he is in 1851 census of Arinagour, Coll aged 44, innkeeper. His w. **Catherine** 40, Margaret 13, Ann 11, Allan 9,Catherine 7, Donald 5 all b. KLN, then George 3 b. Coll. None of these Mull-born ch. will be in **OPR KLN** because of GK.

McLean, Allan (c.1810-1890) mason and wid., he d. aged 80, 12 Apr. 1890, of a cerebral haemorrhage at Bunessan, KLV, us.res. Ardtun, his parents' names unknown to procurator fiscal, George B. Sproat. In view of this unusual lack of knowledge, and fluctuation in occupations at this time, he could be the hawker aged 70 in Eorabus, Ardtun in **CEN KLF 1881**.

Maclaine, Allan (1814-1881) shoemaker claimant to estate of LB, and hereditary heir of entail, he lived at Carriagehill, nr. Paisley in 1841. In 1844 said to be *"the only surviving s. of now dec. Lachlan Maclaine, shoemaker, sometime residing at Dykebar Cottage nr. Paisley, who was s. of Allan Maclaine "late in Scallastle", the s. of Lachlan killed in America, s. of Allan who had "received lands in Mull from his f., Lachlan Mor Maclaine of Lochbuy."* **GRO Box 15, Maclaine Papers. Summons of Reduction & Declarator 1844** He was at 54 George Street, Paisley in 1851. Allan d. at Paisley 15 Apr. 1881 leaving only 1 dau. who worked in a thread factory. His claim to be considered an heir to LB was taken seriously by Murdoch 19th of LB and by his s. Murdoch 20th, who took the trouble to visit Lachlan & Allan (subject of this entry) in Paisley in 1841-2. That Allan had a valid claim was assumed from his f. Lachlan's correspondence with Murdoch Maclaine 19th of LB, who had treated him with the respect and courtesy due to a loser in the matter of the LB inheritance, but no one bothered to look into the LB Charter Room, where, if an archivist had been employed, it might have been found that Allan "late in Scallastle" was the grandson of an illegit. s. of Lachlan Mor of Lochbuy (d.c.1684). It is in cases like this that we must call into question the Gaelic system of reciting genealogies, which all have the same style as that cited above, son of... son of ... son of so-and-so that was in America ... but do not distinguish between lawful and unlawful sons. All 3 Murdochs of Lochbuy genuinely feared that these shoemakers might claim their estate, but nobody was able to tell them of the illegitimacy of the first Allan. Much expense was caused by lawyers who had to consult these false heirs of entail, who did not know themselves, just as the heirs of Gillean Maclaine of Scallastle did not know, that their forebear was a nat. ch. Archy Maclaine of LB, in discussing the entail with Gillean Maclaine, had formulated the caveat that the title could not go to anyone not "in the character of a gentleman". Thus they must have felt threatened by what they thought was a true claim from the shoemaker line. Allan suffered a stroke in the 1860s, his speech and face were distorted, but he was still alive to all the concerns of the LB family, and expected to inherit. Allan d. a 'McLean' at 3 Ralston Square Paisley on 15 Apr. 1881,and his w. **Janet Workman**, was unable to write her name on the certificate. The 'Shoemaker's Claim' to the LB estate presumably died with him, but any intending litigants should heed the various legal cases in **JC/MIP**. No claims against wills have ever succeeded in Mull families. **Box 15, GRO & NAS GD174/2236/29**.

McLean, Allan (1819-1878) from Creich, KLF (**ION OPR**) when he m. **Jane McDonald** 18 May 1853, and was 'of the Sloop Rosina' in the entry for birth of his s. Donald in May 1854. Prob. the same as Allan M. fisherman in **CEN KLF 1851** at Deargphort, step-s. of Lachlan McKinnon, who had m. Marion McKinnon in 1826. In 1871, Allan had become a quarryman, and he and Jane had Donald 16, Rosina 13 (named after his sloop !), Coll (q.v.)11, Marion 9, Hector 6, Jane 3 and John 1. He d. Fionnphort 1878 when he was described as a sub postmaster, m. to Jane Macdonald, and was 64 years old. He d. of cancer of the stomach. His parents' names were given as Hector Maclean, shoemaker & Sarah McKinnon. His s. Donald came from Bournemouth and gave info on Allan's death. In **CEN KLF 1881** Jane, now wid. 50, had become post mistress at Fionnphort. Her s. Coll was ferryman on the Fionnphort to Iona run. Jane d. 1904, aged 75.

Maclaine, Dr Andrew (c.1752-1795) surgeon & cattle dealer in Mull, lived at Pennygown, considered a rich man until he collapsed on his return from cattle markets in 1795, and his death rocked the entire economy of Mull. He married **Janet McLachlan**, sister of Eun McLachlan of Laudale, having 4 known ch. by her – Mary,

Alexander, John, Christian. His dau. Mary (c.1775-1862) m. Donald McLachlan, feuar & innkeeper at Portmore TBR. Dr Andrew also had an illegit.dau. by Margaret McLachlan. See Maclaine, Catharine (c.1785-1864). He took a lease of Pennygown & Leitir 1790 **NAS GD174/935/8** and was building a house at Pennygown in 1794: " *The house is 6 ft high in some parts. I expect it will be sclated before the 1st October...*" **Dr Andrew to Murdoch Maclaine of LB 14 Aug. 1794 NAS GD174/1439/5** He was said to owe Allan McDougall £15,000 in Oct. 1796. **NAS GD174/1329/66** Dr Andrew was the bro. of Dr Donald Maclaine (q.v.) and of Hugh Maclaine (q.v.) vintner in TBR **JC/MIP**

McLean, Andrew (1807-1891) tailor m. to **Sarah McInnes**, formerly to **Isabella McKinnon**, he d. 26 Nov. 1891 at Ardura aged 84 of senile debility, Dugald McPhail, neighbour, giving info at his death. He was bpt. 5 Jul. 1807, s. of Neil McLean & Catherine McInnes in Garmony. He was 'tailor & gamekeeper' in **CEN TRS 1871** at Seannabhail, aged 61 with Sarah 56, Colquhoun s. 18 scholar, Christina dau. 14, Elizabeth Campbell gr.dau. 5, Finlay Campbell gr.s. 3, Alina Campbell gr.dau. 1. GRV at Laggan, Lochbuie: "*In memory of Andrew McLean who died at Ardura 28 November 1891 aged 84, also his son Colquhoun McLean who died at Ardura November 1873 aged 21. Erected by his daughters Isabella & Christina McLean, now in America.*" Marr.: Andrew McLean residing at Laggan and Sarah McInnes of the parish of Morvern were publickly proclaimed...within the Kirk of Kinlochspelve, Sun. 26 Feb. and Sun. 5 March 1843. Isabella b. 1 Dec.1843 at Laggan; Lachlan b. 19 Sep. 1847; Thomas bpt. aged 7 mo. 21 Sep. 1851.Other ch. of Andrew McLean are shown in 1851 census at Faolinmore, TRS when he is 40 and Sarah 36 : Eliza 13 (who m. a Campbell ?), Neil 10, Isabel 7 (these 3 'scholars'); Lachlan 4; Catherine mo., wid. 60 b. MRV; Betsy Livingston servt. 48 b. Dundee. The presence of his 60-year-old bro. John in 1781 is baffling, as Neil M. and Catherine McInnes had a John bpt. 1812. No trace of 1st marr. remains, and he was living alone at Laggan KLS in **CEN KLS 1841**. But Eliza,13 and Neil 10 in 1851, cannot be ch. of Andrew M. and Sarah McInnes. His mo. Catherine, d. at Ardalanish KLF in 1868 when staying with another s., Hector, and her age was then said to be 99, her parents' names Dugald McInnes (mason) and Catherine McInnes. **OPR**

TRS. OPR KLS. CEN KLS 1851, 1861, 1871, 1881, 1891. GVS Laggan.

McLean, Andrew (1814-1891) remained single like most of his siblings, and d. 19 May 1891 at Glenaros aged 77. He was 10th s. of Dr Donald McLaine (q.v.) whose name was spelt that way among LB set, and his w. Mary McNicol, dau. of the min. of Lismore, Donald McNicol. Of his 10 bros., at least 6 are known to have d. young, a strange state of affairs in a medical family. Andrew's cause of death was dropsy. D. McLucas, inmate gave info, and the death was cert. by Duncan McCallum MB.CM. This was the 2nd Andrew bpt. 22 Sep. 1814, so an older bro. bpt. 1796 prob. d. The 1st Andrew had attended Glasgow Univ. *Andreas McLean filius natu primus Donaldi Chirurgi in Insula Mull Argathelia*. Addison matriculations 1811. Many refs to this family in **GRO/LMD** and **JC/MIP**.

McLean, Angus (c.1693-d. >1773) 3rd cousin of Dr Hector McLean of Gruline, mentioned in Boswell's JOURNAL [1773] as " *a tall comely man, a widower, who had been unlucky in the world and now lived among his relations, chiefly with Dr McLean... Though dressed in a shabby kilt with shabby tartan hose, a coat and a waistcoat of coarse dark brown cloth grown old, a wig too little for his head, with no curls, also aged, and a coloured handkerchief about his neck, he had the air of a gentleman. One could not but have a respect for him.*" Angus McLean was then 79.

McLean, Angus (c.1739-1790s) 'The bigamist of Brolass'. According to Presbytery Minutes he was 'husband of the Morvern adulteress **Christian McLean**'. Appeared before the Presbytery of Mull 9 Aug. 1790, having taken a 2nd w. in Kintyre. This aroused some sympathy in the gentlemen of KLF parish, who started a fund to enable him to divorce his first w. The outcome is not known. He was prob. Angus, 40, servant to Alexander McLean, tacksman in Killunaig (later Maclean of Pennycross) in **ERC/Inhabitants 1879**.

McLean, Angus (<1750) in Kilchrist when he m. **Katherine Mcffaiden**, 2 May 1769. Ch. in KLN OPR: fflorence 1772; Duncan 1778; John 1781; Ann 1783; an unnamed dau. 1793 all bpt. at Kilbrenan & Fanmore. The un-named dau. was poss. Catherine who d. as Catherine (husb. John) Lamont in TBR 16 June 1863 aged 68, with these parents' names. **KLN OPR**

McLean, Angus (b.1754) herd in **ERC/Inhabitants 1779** in Gometra, then part of Argyll estates. In **KLN OPR** m. to **fflora McQuary** and living in Gometra. Bpts: Mary 1785; fflora 1789; Christina 1792; John 1795; Ann 1797; Archibald 1799; Catherine 1801. An Angus McLean in Gometra and Ann McDonald had dau. Mary bpt. 5 Jan. 1812, and this might be a 2nd marr.

McLean, Angus (<1780) m. to **Beatrice Fletcher**; lived in Garmony and Scallastle, he had at least 12 ch. bpt. in **TRS OPR**: Mary 1802; n.k. 1804; Charles 1805; John 1807 (all at Garmony). Donald 1809; Duncan 1811; Allan 1814; Anne 1816; Hector 1819; Marion 1821; Allan 1824, Margaret 1826 (all at Scallastle). A 'Rebecca' McLean, 55 in **CEN TRS 1841** at Scallastle, with a Sarah and an Allan, 15, may be his wid. This is a remarkably consistent family, with Beatrice having that name through 12 bpts. till 1826.

McLean, Angus (c.1785-1875) s. of Charles McLean, weaver & Margaret Campbell, he came from Ardtun, Ross of Mull on his marr., 12 Mar. 1812 to **Catherine McLean**, Ardtun. Thereafter their place of abode was referred to as either Torranuachdrach or Killunaig, and Angus was a tenant. Bpts. in **KLF OPR** were Neil 1813, Neil 1814, John 1815, Flora 1817, then a gap before Cirsty 1825 and Margaret 1828. Angus is a wid. in 1871 census at the overpopulated Kinloch aged 85, formerly woollen weaver, and said to have been b. KLN. His dau. Flora is now 51, m. to John McGilvray 62, day lab., with grown-up s. Neil 26. Angus has another gr.s., Donald McDonald 12, scholar. By the time of his death at Kinloch aged 91 on 6 Jun. 1875, Angus was a pauper, so it was the Insp. of the Poor who gave details.

McLean, Angus (c.1788-1879) ploughman at Pennyghael at the time of his marr., 23 Feb.1814, to **Effie McKinnon**, but also described as miller. Bpts. in **KLF OPR** at Killunaig/Pennyghael are of Ann 1814, Donald 1815, Mary 1818, then a gap before John 1825, Hector 1827, John 1829 and Lachlan 1831. According to D. Whyte's *Dictionary of Scottish Emigrants to Canada*, he went from Killunaig to Mariposa Township, Victoria County, Ontario in 1833, but only his w. and s. Lachlan are reported as having gone with him. The names of the other ch. are unfortunately too Macleanish to identify among people who stayed on.

McLean, Angus (<1790) m. **Catherine McPherson**. See McLean, Neil (1809-1883) his s., a fisherman in Tobermory. There are 2 bpts. in

KLN OPR – Neil 1809 & Christina 1810.

McLean, Angus (c.1790-1866) tailor, wid. he d. 2 Mar. 1866 on day following his bro. Alexander (q.v.) Portmore, TBR aged 76, s. of Malcolm McLean (q.v.) householder, and Christina Lamont. In **CEN TBR 1841**, Angus McLean tailor, 40, with Malcolm 15, Ann 8, Lachlan 6, Hugh 4, Peter 2. In **CEN TBR 1851** of Strongarbh it is revealed that Angus was a wid., now 55, tailor, with dau. Ann 20 as housekeeper, sons Hugh 16, Peter 13, 'scholars'. In 1861 Angus is in Strongarbh, 70, with Peter only, now 22 and a tailor. Angus's bp. is Coll, Grimisary.

McLean, Angus (c.1797-1867) s. of Neil McLean (q.v.) & Flora McKinnon, he was shepherd in Torrans, KLF, and d. wid. of Flora McDougall 10 Nov. 1867 aged 70 at Torrans. Flora d. between 1851 and 1861. Their ch. in **CEN KLF 1841** were Flora 16, Catherine 14, Ann 3, Isabella 18 mo.; **CEN KLF 1851** adds Alexander (c.1842), Catherine (c.1842), Marion (c.1845) and Cirsty (c.1850). Absence of bpts. in **KLF OPR** suggest that this family were adherents of FC or Baptists. Their dau. Ann m. John McGillivray, and d. Iona aged 50 in 1889 of scarlet fever.

McLaine, Rev. Angus (1800-1877) 2nd s. of Allan Maclaine (q.v.) of Scallastle and Marjory Gregorson. His f., soon to be judged mentally disturbed, tried to take him from his mo. when he was an infant. Marjory was given judicial custody of the 2 boys, who showed great promise at Glasgow Univ. His bro. Gillean, who had made money in a Java coffee business was tragically drowned with his w. and family, and Angus, then min. of Ardnamurchan, inherited a large amount of money. Angus inherited business interests and property in Java and bought land at Ardtornish (now S. Australia) visiting Australia in the 1830s and 'bushing it' or bivouacing among aborigines, about whom he wrote home. He devoted his legacy to charitable causes, mainly among the poor of Mull. He never m., and was paraplegic for 20 years < he d. 20 Dec. 1877 at the Queens Hotel, George Street, Glasgow aged 77, his us. res. Fascadale, Argyllshire. He was custodian of the large collection of family papers belonging to his gr.f. Gillean Maclaine of Scallastle, and on his death these passed to his cousin, W. Maclaine, of Thornbury, Gloucestershire, and are now in **GRO/Glouc**.

McLean, Angus (c.1800-1852) "*Angus McLean Tavool died Sept.1852. His wife* **Jane McLean**

died 9 January 1901 aged 89, also their two daughters Catherine and Kate who predeceased them." **GRV Killiemore KLF. CRD** has his death as 1855 aged 53, bearing out the caveat in the preface to this book about GRV inscriptions. Angus was in **CEN KLF 1841** at Tavool (Tapull, Ardmeanach – formerly part of LB estate) aged 35, cottar, with Jane 25, Sally 4 and John 1. He was in **CEN KLF 1851** at Tavool aged 44, dyke builder, b. Pennygown, with his w. Jane 37, b. TRS, and 4 ch. – Sally 14, John 11, Chirstie 7 and Duncan 1, all b. Ardmeanach. But CRD 1855 of Angus shows 2 ch., Catherine & Cate had d. at 9 and 7. In 1855 Sally was 18, John 16, Duncan 5, Ann 3.

Maclean, Angus (c.1785-1875) pauper, wid. of **Catherine McLean**, d. 6 Jun. 1875 at Kinloch aged 91. Parents were Charles Maclean weaver & Margaret Campbell and he d. of 'general decay' according to Insp. of Poor, Bunessan. In **CEN KLF 1871** at Kinloch, Angus is 85, and lives with his s.-in-law John McGillvray 62, dau. Flora 51, and gr.s. Neil McGillivray 26 and Donald McDonald, 12. His marr. to Catherine was 12 Mar. 1812 when he was from Ardtun and she from Killunaig. Ch. in **KLF OPR** were Neil 1813, Neil 1814, John 1815, Flora 1817, Cirsty 1825, Margaret 1828. In these years Angus was a tenant at Torranuachdrach.

McLean, Ann (<1785) sister of Charles, Neil, Lachlan and Catherine McLean, dau. of Duncan McLean and Mary McLean, she m. **Duncan McKechnie**, formerly McEachern, <1804, and they were in Fidden KLF < twins Duncan & Ann were bpt. 28 Dec. 1804. They make no further appearance in Mull OPRs, and were in Port Bannatyne, nr. Rothesay, Isle of Bute, in 1841, but as descendant of John Og McLean in Fishnish, Ann received legacy from the Will of her cousin, Miss Mary McLean (q.v.) matron of the Town's Hospital, Glasgow, who d. 1834.

McLean, Ann (c.1790-1886) pauper, wid. of **John McLean**, pensioner, she d. aged 97, 10 Sep.1886, at Ardtun, KLF, the info given by Alexander McGregor, Insp. of Poor being that her f. was Lachlan McInnes farmer, and her mo. Catherine McPhail. She d. after 2 yrs. of 'gradual exhaustion' as cert. by her doctor, Alexander MacKechnie, GP, Bunessan. It was he who is said to have advised all Mull McEacherns to change their names to MacKechnie if they wanted to get on in life.

McLean, Ann (c.1792-1880), wid. of **Donald McLean** (b.c.1792, q.v.), farmer, dau. of Dugald

MacArthur & Ann McCormick, she d. at Kintra aged 88, of old age.

McLean, Ann (c.1799-1888) dau. of Lachlan McLean crofter & Catherine McLean M/S McLean, wid. of **Duncan McLean**, crofter at Kinloch, she d. of 'general decay' as cert. by Dr MacKechnie, aged 87, 28 Dec. 1888 at Kinloch. Allan McLean, her s. was present.

McLean,'Lady' Annabella (1776-1855) dau. of Archibald McLean of Kilmoluaig, Tiree, she was b. there, her mo. being Catherine Campbell, dau. of Donald Campbell of Scammadale. See **AMS/CG p.324**. She d. at Gowanbrae, Bunessan, single, aged 79, 26 Apr. 1855 of senile gangrene. She was a sister of John McLean, f. of Sir Donald McLean, NZ. The use of 'Lady' reflects her prestige in the community, and perhaps her social manner, and was not uncommon in describing tacksmen's wives and daus.

McLean, Ann (bpt.1815) A considerable amount of detective work has been required to root out the story of this unfortunate, twice-widowed woman, destined to be a pauper in Shiaba, KLF. Her parents, John McLaine & Helen McLaine m. in Fishnish on the day Ann was bpt. Her f. John d. of consumption at Fishnish in 1825 *"leaving a widowed mother childless and a young weak family off our orphans, two boys and two girls."* **GRO LMD**. In **LMD/Souls** at Fishnish in 1829, Helen was 34, Ann 14, Archibald 12, Lachlan 12, and Ann's younger sister Helen 7. Ann m. a **McKinnon** c.1835 when about 20, but her husb. d. perhaps in early 1840s, and she m. a **McArthur**. c.1844. 3 McArthur ch.were b. – Mary c.1845, Margaret c.1847, and John 1850. Again Ann was widowed, and in **CEN KLF 1851** she is to be found in Shiaba KLF aged 34, already a pauper, with her mo. Helen, 55, likewise a pauper, her dau. Ann McKinnon 15, and her 3 McArthurs, Mary, Margaret and John. Worse was probably to befall her, as Shiaba township was cleared both < and > 1851. She was what Mull people called an 'object' – someone very poor, pathetic and pitiable.

Maclean, Anne (c.1825-1909) d. Langamull 1909 aged 84, w. of the late **Coll Maclean. GRV KLN** – for whole inscription see Maclean, Charles (c.1793-1866) her f.

McLean, Ann (c.1826-1876) m. to **Alexander McLean**, lab. she d. Fanmore KLN 1876 aged 50, dau. of Neil McLean & a Campbell mo. whose Christian name is missing in **CRD** info given by a

relative, Archibald McLaine.

McLean, Ann (c.1857-1897) single, nurse, dau. of Hugh McLean seaman & Catherine McInnes, she d. aged 40 of cardiac arrest when walking on public road near Kilfinichen Ho. Dr Duncan McDonald MB.CM. Salen attended; info from Procurator Fiscal.

McLean, Anny (fl.1740s-1760s) dau. of Allan McLean of Kilmory, she went to Edinburgh to be instructed in the thread business by **James Spalding**, and m. him. Her bro. was Murdoch McLean of Kilmory, and she was also related to Torloisks or Lochbuys, as Murdoch Maclaine 19th of LB was involved with Bonnymilns, run by Spaldings. Anny's marr. contract is in NAS GD174/2054.

McLean, Annie Fraser (c.1874-1904)m. to **Dugald McLean**, seaman mate d. 30 Apr. 1904 at Argyll Hotel, Iona, aged 29, of puerperal septicoma, att. by George Edgar MB. Her f. was James McKay, gardener, her mo. Isabella Fraser. Dugald McLean, wid. on board SS Lochiel gave info.

McLean, Annie Fraser (b. and d. 1904) infant dau. of above, she d. aged 27 days at Argyll Hotel Iona 22 May 1904, f. Dugald McLean seaman mate; mo. Annie Fraser McLean, dec. Info from her cousin Archibald McArthur,Clachanach, Iona.

McLean, Mr Archibald (1679-1755) In these days the designation 'Mr' usually denoted a min., or univ.-educated man. This min. was in Ross of Mull from 1720, and is incl. in this collection as ancestor of Ardfenaig Macleans and others. See **FASTI**. He m. 1722 **Susanna Campbell**, dau. of Donald Campbell of Scammadale, sister of 'Lady' Annabella McLean's mo. Ch. listed in **AMS/CG**, but Margaret, b. 1737 m. the Rev. Neil Macleod, min. of KLF & KLV, and was commended by Dr Johnson for knowing how to be a min.'s w. Margaret's dau. Susanna Macleod m. Capt. Dugald McLean of Ardfenaig (q.v.).

McLean, Archibald (18th C.) surgeon b. Mull, practised in Jamaica. His Will, dated 1772 is in **LBP NAS GD174/159**. 5 sisters are legatees: Euphemia w. of Donald McLean in Mull; Mary w. of John McLean in Mull; Ann w. of Allan McLean in Mull; Margaret single – in Banffshire; Sarah single, of Mull. Executors incl. Donald Campbell of Airds & John Campbell of Ardtornish.

McLean, Archibald (c.1727-1781) 4th s. of Donald Maclean (q.v.) of Torloisk, was unm.

mercht. in Lagganulva, and managed estate of Torloisk in absence of his older bros. the lairds Hector & Lachlan McLean. He had a relationship with Marion McLean, by whom he had a s. John (1755-1821) of Kilbrenan & dau. Alice, so that **AMS**'s assertion that he had no issue is not valid. **AMS/CG** says he was "*a kind-hearted man, the author of several Gaelic songs*", but evidence in **GRO** and **TP** would suggest he was extremely difficult, a womaniser, a troublemaker, and **MPM** show him to be a "*quadrelapse in fornication*." "*As he knows McQ's weak side he cringes and fawns like a spaniel to curry favour with him and Mrs McQ... Mally never speaks to him...*" NAS **GD174/1244/31; JC/MIP** His death date is problematical. **AMS/CG** gives 1800, but other evidence in **GD174/1329/17** suggests 1781. If 1781 is correct 'Cousin' Donald McLean was referring to Archy Laggan's nat. ch. when he said, "*Mr Colquhoun Grant tells me there was a strong will in favour of his son & daughter*."

McLean, Archibald (1733-1812) Bapt.min. b. E.Kilbride of Mull stock. *Dict. of Scottish Church History & Theology*.

McLean, Archibald (<1740) in Glenforsa, on LB estate, he m. **Mary McLean**, who, according to **MPM** claimed in 1776 that she had borne a s. to John Maclaine (q.v.) tacksman of Gruline about 12 years earlier, who had been passed off as her husb.'s own s. Evidence in **LBP** of John Gruline being blackmailed. As bpts. in Glenforsa were kept by the Mull Mission, and are lost, we cannot identify this boy, b. 1764.

McLean, Archibald (fl. 1740-1784) m. **Ann McNeill**, lived at Sorn of Mishnish. Bpts. to this couple in **KLN OPR**: Donald 1766, Neil 1769, fflorence 1771, John 1777, Marion 1780, Duncan 1784.

McLean, Archibald (fl.1740s-1770s) m. **Janet Livingston**, lived in Drimgigha, Langamull and Kildavee. Bpts. in **KLN OPR**: Alexander 1768, Mary 1772, Archibald 1775.

Maclaine, Archibald (1749-1784) 18th of LB, 'Archy Lochbuy' s. of John Maclaine (q.v.) & Isabel Maclean of Brolass; he was laird conjointly with his f., but estate was in debt, and he made an entail, abetted by his half-brother Gillean (q.v.) in an attempt to find ready cash. He went to America at outbreak of revolutionary war, m. Barbara Lowther in 1784, but was murdered on board ship returning to Britain from Jamaica. Full account in **JC/MIP**

McLean, Archibald (fl.1750s-1803) m. **fflora McDonald**, 4 Dec. 1777, lived in Burg, KLN. Bpts. in KLN OPR: Donald 1780, Hugh 1782, Archibald 1793, Marion 1795, Christina 1797, Lauchlan 1799, Donald 1803.

Maclean, Archibald (1761-1830) 2nd of Pennycross, only s. of Dr Alexander Maclean (q.v.) of PX & Una McGillivray. He m. **Alice**, dau. of Hector Maclean (q.v.) of Torranbeg and Julian McLean with 9 ch. – Alexander (q.v.) 1791, Allan Thomas (q.v.) 1793, Charles James, Mary, John, Julian (c.1797-1874), Hector (d.1834), Lachlan (d.1830) Archibald Donald (q.v.) Deputy Commissioner in Bermuda, unm.

McLean, Archibald (c.1767-1860), wid., d. 1860 at Ardchiavaig aged 93, s. of Hector McLean, crofter & Catherine McDonald. His s. Hector gave info on his death. His marr. in **KLF OPR** to **Cirsty McEachern** was 12 Mar. 1811, when he was a crofter in Uisken, and she lived in Ardalanish. Bapts – Alexander 1811, Effy 1813, Lachlan 1814, Hector 1819, another Lachlan 1826. The family is in **CEN KLF 1851** at Ardchiavaig when Archibald was recorded as being "in receipt of alms" aged 80. His w. was 68, and his s. Hector 32,a fisherman, was m. to a Ketty [McInnes, b.Coll] with a 2-year-old Ketty. Archibald's bro. d. 1861 in Iona aged 91, and it is possible that the Hector McLean in **ERC/Inhabitants** in Iona, b.c. 1739 was the f. After Archibald's death, his s. Hector continued in the croft, but was a pauper in 1871. His bro. Lachlan, visiting in 1871 with Andrew 5 and Christina 3, had sensibly migrated to Glasgow.

Maclean, Archibald (1777-1856) s. of Hector Maclean from Achronich KLN & Flory or Florence Cameron, he was bpt. Kilbrenan 9 Feb. 1777, m. a **Marion**, and is in Balligown 1851 aged 80 with 'Merron' 70, Flora 40, John 30 & dau. 'Merron' 25. He d. 15 Jun. 1856, age still 80, at Balligown in presence of his dau. 'Marron'. Details of this family lost in GK.

Maclaine, Sir Archibald (1777-1861) twin s., with Murdoch, of Gillean Maclaine (q.v.) & Marie McQuarrie, he was b. at Scallastle. He served in the army (94th Regt) settled in England after the French wars ceased, and m. in 1823 **Elizabeth Brydges**, but their only s. died in infancy. He had had a nat. s. in 1806, Colin Campbell Maclaine (q.v.), by Mary Fletcher in Ledirkle. His own old nurse, Marion McLean, d. in abject poverty in 1829, for which Sir Archibald was criticised by his half-bro. Lauchlan Maclaine (q.v.) *"Many a time from my heart have I cried shame upon Archy when I have gone into her house and witnessed her wants. Had he not promised to give her £5 a year during her life, matters would have been less thought of. The poor husband frequently wrote him, but received neither answer nor money."* The name of the husb. was Malcolm Currie. **GRO. Letter to Margaret Craig. 1830. JC/M1P**

McLean, Archibald (<1780) his death reported in Iona OPR 21 Mar. 1848. *"Archibald McLean, Elder, Creich, died suddenly this morning having been in his usual health at time of going to bed."* 10 days later another entry: *"***Mary McDonald,*** wife of the above Archibald McLean, died, having never awoke after a dose of laudanum having been administered to her by Dr Beveridge."*

McLean, Archibald (c.1780–1817) of Scour KLV. 'Gilleasbuig na Sgurra', s. of Charles Maclean & Catherine Maclean of Muck, gr.s. of Mr Archibald, min. of Ross. Served in 71st & 79th regiments. Retired from military 1807, d. unm. 1817, but had a nat. child, Lavinia McLean by Marion McLean in Ardfenaig bpt. 12 Sep. 1817. According to *Na Baird Thirisdeach*, he was a splendid soldier, a gallant officer, loved by his men, and a Gaelic lament by John McLean bears this out.

McLean, Archibald (fl.1780-1825) m. when in Braes of Lagganulva, **Marion Campbell**, 2 Apr. 1805. Lived at Stronbuy. Bpts. in KLN OPR: Ann 1811, Catherine 1813, John 1816, Marion 1823, Mary 1825.

McLean, Archibald (fl. 1780s-1820s) m. **Mary McLean**. Bpts. in KLN OPR: Alexander 1811 at Kilbrenan, John 1815 at K., Neil 1819 at Balligown, Mary 1821 at Langamull.

McLean, Archibald (c.1791-1840s) of Uisken, army pensioner aged 50 in **CEN KLF 1841**, with 'Mrs McLean' 35, Lilly 16 & Peggy 1. **KLN OPR** has marr. 1820 of Lieut. Archibald to **Sarah McPherson** in Corkamull, but another record has different date. Lilly was bpt. Lagganulva KLN 1823. They lived at Uisken KLV and bpts. in **KLF OPR** are of Mary 1823, John 1827, Donald 1829, Mary 1831, and a surprisingly late Margaret in 1846. A s., John Ralph Abercromby McLean (the John of 1827), re-appears as med.stud. in Glasgow in connection with the claim against the Will of Archibald's bro. Alexander McLean (q.v.). **GRO Testament of Lt.-Col. Alexander McLean**. His descendants remain untraced, and **AMS/CG** states that John Ralph (d. unm. 1903) was last representative of the family. This ignores possible descendants in the female line.

McLean, Archibald (c.1791) m. **Mary McDonald** and lived in Saorphein KLF where in **CEN KLF 1841** we find him aged 55 with Mary 50, and Ewen (= Hugh) 10, the only ch. from 10 bpts. in **KLF OPR** still at home. The other ch. were Janet b.1809, unnamed 1811, Catherine 1813, John 1815, Mary 1817, Ann 1820, Neil 1823, Mary 1825, John 1828. Duplication of names suggests at least 1 John and 1 Mary had d.

McLean, Archibald (fl.1800-1826) gardener at Penmollach, Maclean of Coll's estate, lived later at Dervaig, m. **Ann McKinnon** Penmollach 2 Nov. 1824. GRV Kilmore commemorates his w.: *"Erected by John McLean in memory of his mother Ann McKinnon, wife of AM, gardener, Penmollach who died [illeg. date] and her daughter Mary McLean"*.In **CEN KLN 1861** he was in Penmollach KLM aged 56 with Ann 60, Mary their marr. dau. 32, John McLean their s.-in-law 30 b. Coll, and gr.daus. Catherine 3 and Ann 10 mos. **GRV Kilmore** (Dervaig).

McLean, Archibald (c.1805-1865) s. of Hector McLean, blacksmith & Jessie McNeill, he became a tailor in Tavool KLF, m.**Christian McNeill**, (McNeills were very given to marrying each other). He was a pauper in 1851 aged 50, and in this hard economic time, so were 4 of his ch. – Janet 9, Cirsty 7, Charles 5, Neil 2. His s. Colin, 16, laboured on the roads, and must have supported entire family. His dau. Janet was blind, so remained on Poor Roll, and in 1861 he had 3 more ch. – Effy, Angus and John. Archy McLean d. at Tavool 26 Dec. 1865 aged 65 of a malignant sore throat, his nephew Archibald McNeill being present at his death. In 1871 his wid. Christina was at Tavool Cottage with Cirsty 27, now a dressmaker, John 11 and her gr.dau. Sarah McLean aged 1.

Maclean, Archibald Donald (1802-1870) d. unm. at Carsaig aged 68, 16 Nov. 1870. He had been Dep. Asst.Commissary General [Navy Office] on half pay, the youngest, and apart from his sister Julia, the longest surviving of the ch. of Archibald Maclean (q.v.) of PX & Alicia Maclean M/S Maclean. His cause of death 'malignant ulceration of the mouth' cert. by Dr Donald Black MB.

McLean, Archibald (bpt. 13 Oct. 1805) – or perhaps the right to baptism was obtained for him in an incident in Kilninian Kirk when his gr.f. became his sponsor. The ch. was nat. s. of 'Marey', dau. of

John McLean (q.v.) schoolmaster in Balligown, and Marey must also have been 'natural'.Archibald McColl protested against the baptism by taking instruments of baptism from the Beadle.

McLean, Archibald (c.1808) handloom weaver of wool, m. to **Flory Buchanan** (1805-1860).In **CEN KLN 1841** Dervaig he is 40 with Flora 35, Mary 6, Bell 4, John 1. In 1851 Dervaig he is 42, b. KLN with Flora 42, Mally 14, Isabella 13, John 9, Anne 7 – all scholars; Neil 5.

McLean, Archibald (c.1824) fisherman in Kilninian m. **Mary McInnes** Dec. 1849 KLN, and in **CEN KLN 1851** at Kilninian he was f. of 6-year-old John, s.-in-law of John McInnes 75.

Maclean, Archibald John (1843-1899) 4th of Pennycross, s. of Sandy PX & Charlotte Brodie Maclean, succeeded 1876 to estate in parlous state of debt, and sold in 1888. He m. 1868 **Isabella Alexandrina Simon** (q.v. **under** Maclean) who d. 1886. He continued to live in Mull, at Tiroran, after selling PX.

McLean, Archibald (b. 1816) s. of Duncan and Janet McLeans, Drimgigha. KLN OPR See article by Duart Allan Maclean, *A Family Emigration from the Isle of Mull to Canada in 1843* in *Notes & Queries XIV December 1980*.

McLean, Archibald (c.1827-1860) d. single, farmer, aged 33 at Penmore KLN, 1860 s. of Charles McLean (q.v.) & Mary McLucash. He was bro. of Patrick or Peter McLean (q.v.), boatman.

McLean, Archibald (c.1805-1872) feuar, contractor, joiner, unm., d. 12 Nov. 1872 at Portmore TBR aged 67, s. of John McLean, farmer & Margaret McLean M/S McCallum of 'gastronomic difficulties'. His sister Flora McKinnon grocer Portmore gave info.

McLean, Beatrice bpt. 16 Mar. 1800, dau. of John McLean, soldier, and Mary McLean, Fishnish. **TRS OPR**

McLean, Betsy (1843-1923) dau. of shepherd John Clark & Janet McPherson, she d. at Glenforsa aged 78 in 1923. See **McLean, Hector** (c.1843-1915), her husb. for description of her attractive personality & appearance.

McLean, Betty (c.1798-1870) pauper, wid. of **Archibald McLean**, she d. of emphysema at Uisken 1870, aged 72, dau. of John McLean, weaver & Margaret Macdonald.

McLean, Breadalbane (b.1793) unm. dau. of Alexander Maclean of Coll & Catherine Cameron, was bpt. at Inveresk27 Nov. 1793, brought up partly at Quinish and devoted her life to doing good. With a small house of her own at Dervaig, Retreat Cottage, she was able to return to Mull even after her bro. Hugh had gone to live in London, but also let it frequently when she was in Kensington, living on a small annuity. Several Mull girls were named after her, including Breadalbane, dau. of Donald Maclean, gardener in Dervaig.

McLean, Carnegie (fl.1768) engraver referred to in letters in **NAS/GD174/1264/15** as s. of a John McLean. "*I know that John McLean has a son that is ane engraver. Whether his name be Carnegie or not I cant say*." A Carnegie Maclean, engraver & **Isobel**, dau. of Thomas **Morison**, mariner in Stirling, were m. in Edinburgh Tron Parish 25 Nov. 1764.

McLean, Catherine (fl.1710-1780s) dau. of Donald McLean of Coll (1656-1729), she m. **Dr Hector McLean** of Gruline possibly c.1738, her dau. 'Miss McLean' being b. c.1740. '*A little brisk old woman in a bed gown*' according to James Boswell. **JC/MIP**

Maclaine, Catherine (1750s-1828) dau. of John Maclaine of LB & Isobel Maclean of Brolass, she m. Hugh McGilvra of Pennyghael in 1778, and had 1 s. Alexander McGilvra with whose death in 1864 unm. the old PG territorial title became extinct. Her McGilvra daus. were Isabella, Una & Catherine. Her relations with the LBs were embittered by a 50-year struggle for a marr. portion.

McLean, Catherine (c.1769-1859) wid. of a farmer, she d. 27 Jan. 1859 at Village Iona, aged 90, dau. of Donald McLean farmer & Mary McLean M/S McLean. Bur. Relig Oran, Iona. Hugh McLean, s.-in-law, gave info for **CRD**. This was wid. of **Lachlan McLean**. Their dau. Euphemia m. Hugh McLean, mercht.

McLean, Catherine (c.1779-1859) wid., pauper, she d. aged 80 on 8 Apr. 1859 at Torrans dau. of John McLean crofter & Mary McLean M/S McLean of a pulmonary disease, according to D. Graham, Insp. of Poor.

McLean, Catherine (b. 18th C.) dau. of Hector McLean in Glenbyre & Flora McLean, gr.dau. of Neil McLean in Fishnish, she m. Neil Carmichael, sometime in Ardchrishnish. The only record found for her and her husb. in OPR is bpts. of a s. John Carmichael at Glenbyre in 1805. Catherine as wid.was benficiary in the Will of her cousin Miss Mary McLean (q.v.) matron of the Town's

24

Hospital, Glasgow, who d. 1834.

McLean, Catherine (1785-1875) dau. of Duncan McLean of Uisken & Mary McLean, sister of Lt-Col. Alexander McLean (q.v.) of Uisken, she m. **Hugh Fletcher**, overseer in Fidden KLF, later in Tirghoil KLF in 1809. Their ch. were Catherine 1810, Janet 1813, Alexander 1814, John 1816, Elizabeth 1818, Dugald Stewart 1820, Julian (girl) 1822, Duncan 1824, Charles 1827. The family left for Canada, possibly after the death of Hugh Fletcher in the 1840s, and the friendship of Charles with a Bunessan school friend, Charles Macquarie provides us with a correspondence which has survived between them in which Macquarie describes events in the Ross of Mull in the famine years. Catherine was one of those who challenged the will of her uncle, Lieut.-Col. Alexander McLean when he left most of his fortune for the education of Maclean boys.

McLaine, Catherine (c.1785-1864) d. High Street, Tobermory (a.k.a. McKenzie Street) 25 Jan. 1864, wid. of **Charles McLaine** [sic] feuar, at the age of 79. In CRD her f.'s name is Andrew McLaine surgeon, Pennygown, and her mo. is Margaret McLachlan and Catharine is illegit. This makes her the dau. of one of the key characters in Mull history. Dr Andrew McLaine (q.v.) was a drover as well as a surgeon, and rocked the economy of Mull by his sudden death as he returned from the cattle markets of 1795. For her husb. see McLean, Charles (c.1780-1857) and for her f. see McLaine, Andrew (d.1795) and **JC/MIP** p.163.

McLean, Catherine (<1795) m. **John McArthur** tenant in Glenforsa c.1840. She was one of 10 legatees in Will of her cousin Miss Mary McLean (q.v.) matron of the Town's Hospital, Glasgow, who d. 1834. She was a dau. of Duncan McLean & Mary McLean, Duncan McLean being a s. of Neil McLean in Fishnish TRS. But although we know her bros. were John McLean carpenter in Greenock & Neil & Lachlan McLean, tenants in Scobull, no other details of her have emerged, and one can only guess that she was b. in the 1790s.

McLean, Catherine (1791-1865) b. Arinagour, Coll, she m. **Hector McKinnon** (1771-1837) of Derriguaig in Mull, and through her dau. Isabella was gr.mo. of the ch. of Neil Whiteside Maclean (q.v.) She d. Geelong, Victoria, Australia.

Maclaine, Catherine (1793-1894) single, d. 6 Apr. 1894 aged 97 [incorrect] dau. of Murdoch Maclaine (q.v.) of LB & Jane Campbell of heart disease and fracture of the thigh. Info. Janet Currie Lochbuy. This was 'Miss Catherine', once a scatty young girl who stayed in London with her aunt, Elizabeth Henrietta Macquarie, w. of Lachlan Macquarie of NSW. **JC/MIP**

McLean, Catherine (1860-1861) infant dau. of John McLean (q.v.) miller at Penmore & Catherine McMaster, she d. 23 May 1861 in a drowning accident.

McLean, Catherine See **McLean Neil** (c. 1809-1883) fisherman in Tobermory, her husb.

McLean, Catherine (c.1792-1880) dau. of Neil McKinnon & Flora Morrison, wid. of **John McLean** miller at Penmore, she d. 11 Jan. 1880 aged 88. Her gr.son Alexander McLean gave info. She was gr.mo. of the baby girl Catherine who d. 1861.

McLean, Catherine (c.1805-1889) dau. of Robert Lamont mercht. and Hannah McLean, she d. 3 May 1889 at Iona, aged 84, m. to **Hector McLean**, crofter, George Ritchie ["mother's sister's..." scored out, but significant] bro.-in-law, gave info.

Maclean, Catherine (c.1826-1905) b. Barra, dau. of John McNeill, fisherman & Marion McNeill, M/S McNeill, she was m. to **Donald MacLean** (q.v.) crofter, Fanmore KLN, and d. of old age at 79 in 1905. Her s. George McLean, gave info.

McLean, Catherine (c.1842-1902) housewife m. to **Dugald McLean**, ploughman, she d. aged 60, 28 Apr. 1902 at Torrans KLF; her parents were John McKinnon, blacksmith, and Mary McGillivray.

McLean, Charles (b.<1740) m. to **Catherine McKenzie**; lived in Drimnacroish & Aintuim KLN. Bpts. twins Hector & Donald 15 Apr. 1769; Hugh8 May 1782; Duncan 22 Jul. 1784.

McLean, Charles (b.<1740s) m. **Isobel McGilvray** at Goirtengoy; their dau. Grizel bpt. 1772; their dau. Christian bpt. at Teang 1774; s. Duncan at Bainachdrach 1779; s. Roderick bpt. 1782. **KLN OPR**.

McLean, Charles (b.c.1750) m. 2 Feb. 1775 in Gometra, **Elspet** (sometimes Elizabeth) **McQuary**. Their dau. Catherine was bpt. in Gometra 19 May 1776 **KLN OPR**

McLean, Charles (b. c.1750) m. 12 Dec. 1775, when he was from Coll, **Catherine Paterson KLN OPR** Bpts.: John 18 Jan. 1778 at Aintuim; Flora 25 Mar. 1780 at Aintuim; James 11 Jan.

1784 in Torasa KLN.

McLean, Charles (bpt. 30 Jan. 1767) s. of John McLean (q.v.) & Effy Stewart in Acharn, KLN . In **ERC/Inhabitants 1779** at Acharn a John McLean aged 50 is a tenant with a 10-year-old s. Charles. Charles was f. of Rev. Neil McLean of Ulva, who was b. in 1797, and at least 4 daus. His w. was **Euphemia Campbell** (in some records Isabella). He lived on the mainland for some years, but went to stay at Ulva when his s. became min. there. A description of the Rev. Neil's family in **GRO LMD** 1836: "*his father is a sensible prudent old man, the mother a pleasant garrulous old woman, and the three daughters Helen, Sophy and Mary well-bred good-looking girls all brought up to the millinery business.*" Mary later m. Roderick Morrison – see McLean, Margaret (b.1772)

McLean, Charles (<1770) m. **Marion (Sarah) Currie**; lived in Cameron TRS. Bpts.: Lachlan 1794; Donald 1795; Duncan 1797; Catherine 1802. See also McLaine, John (c.1791-1856) their s.

McLean, Charles (1772->1829) shepherd in Ledirkle TRS, near present-day Fishnish ferry; also spelt Maclaine, m. **Cirsty Campbell** or **Cirsty Black** or both. See Maclaine, Donald (1795-1855) his s. In **LMD/Souls** 1829 there are 22 Maclaines at Ledirkle incl. Charles 57 with w. 54 followed by Donald 36 (an age which fits perfectly with CRD), Murdoch 32 and Janet 20.

McLean, Charles (c.1772) also spelt MacLaine m. **Cirsty Black**. Bpts. in **TRS OPR** at Fishnish, Murdoch 1795 and at Ledirkle Catherine 1797; Mary 1800; John 1803;n.k. 1805; Janet 1806. Another s. Donald McLaine (q.v.) (1793-1855) not in OPR. Family is in **LMD/Souls** 1829 at Ledirkle when Charles is 57, his w. 54, Donald 36, Murdoch 32, Janet 20.

McLean, Charles (<1775) his marr. entry: "*17 Apr. 1798 Charles McLean from Craignish &* **Catherine McNeill** *Balligown were, in the presence of a company of their friends of each side, married.*" **KLN OPR**. An unusually formal and elegant manner of recording a marr. An Iver, sometimes called Edward, McNeill & Flora Cameron, also known as Matthewson, in Tostary had had a dau. Catherine bpt. May 1781.

McLean, Charles (c.1780-1857) s. of Duncan McLean & Mary McLean and gr.s. of Neil McLean in Fishnish, he was one of the beneficiaries in the Will of his cousin, Miss Mary McLean, matron of the Town's Hospital, Glasgow,

who d. 1834. The executry, dated 1834-41 tells us he was 'tenant in Ardmore' but subsequent correspondence might allow us to identify him with Charles McLean in Reraig, nr. Ardmore in 1841 who had m. **Catharine McLaine** and whose s. Duncan was bpt. at Tobermory in 1816. Some of his other ch. (John, Archibald, Mary) were listed in **CEN TOB 1851** when he was a tailor in McKenzie Street aged 70, b. TRS. His w. had an interesting history which is given in the entry for Catherine McLaine (c.1785-1864). He d. 1857 aged 77.

McLean, Charles (<1780) m. **Isabella Campbell** according to CRD of their dau. Jessie McLean (c.1801-1883) who d. at Portmore, Tobermory 19 May 1883 aged 82 of old age. Jessie's nephew who gave info when she d., was Dugald Campbell, JP for Argyll.

McLean, Charles (c.1782-1855) farmer, he d. Kinloch (b. Ormaig) 27 Jan. 1855, aged 73, having lived for 48 yrs. in Kinloch KLF. His parents were Allan McLean farmer and Ann McQuarrie. Neil McLean, his s., who signed X gave info. His 1st w. was **Mary McLean M/S McLean** by whom he had Neil 49; John 46; Lachlan 44; Alexander 42; Effy 40; Ann 38; Allan 36; Catherine 34. Secondly he m. **Mary McDonald** (still living when Charles d.) with no issue.These ages are in 1855.

McLean, Charles (c.1783-1863) s. of Malcolm McLean (q.v.) feuar in Tobermory & Chirsty Lamont, he was single and a pauper when he d. 14 Feb. 1863 at Ledag, TBR aged 80. His nephew John McLean gave info for CRD.

McLean, Charles (<1785) packet-master on Quinish-Coll crossing, he m. 27 Feb. 1807 **Flora McLean. KLN OPR**

McLean, Charles (<1785) crofter in Ardtun he m. **Catherine Stewart** <1808. 9 ch. in **KLF OPR**: Mary 1808, twins Donald & John on 8 Nov. 1811, Mary 1813, John 1815, Archibald 1817, Janet 1819, Alexander 1821, Marion 1824. The family disappears from Ardtun after this.

McLean, Charles (c.1793-1866) m. **Mary Livingston**; see McLean, John, d. 1855 aged 19, his s. GRV in Kilninian: "*erected by Donald McLean, Tostary in memory of his father Charles McLean who died at Tostary 1886 aged 73; his mother Mary Livingston who died at Tobermory March 1879 aged 78; his brother John who died at Burg October 1855 aged 18; his brother Peter* *who died at Reudle March 1841 aged 18 months, his sister Anne died at Langamull June 1909 aged 84, wife of the late Coll Maclean (q.v.). In loving memory of Donald Maclean originally of Tostary who died at Langamull on 2nd February 1910 in his 78th year*." Marr. of CM and Mary Livingstone Raodle: 24 Aug. 1824 suggests date on GRV must be 1866, not 1886, so that Charles would be b. 1793 as he couldn't be m. aged 11. **CEN KLN 1861** he is at Tostary aged 67 with Mary 60, his unm. s. John joiner; Allan s., unm. 21. Charles's parents were John McLean crofter & Anne McLean M/S McLean. In **CEN KLN 1851** he is described as a tailor with his sons : John 21, Donald (q.v.)19, Hector 17, John 14, Allan 12. He gave info twice when his v. young gr.-ch. from his dau. Anne d. 1857 and in CRD of his s. John in 1855. His s. Allan d. 1880 at Kilninian, aged 41, husb. of Sarah Henderson.

McLean, Charles m. **Isabella Campbell** See McLean, Jessie (c.1801-1883) his dau., who d. Portmore, single, in 1883.

McLean, Charles m. **Marion Currie**; see his s. Hugh McLean, weaver & pauper, d. 13 Apr. 1860 at Tobermory.

McLean, Charles see Mary McLean who d. at Ledirkle 1860 aged 50.

McLean, Charles (b.1790s) Penmore boatman, he came from Drumgigha and m. **Mary McLucash** in Penmore 4 Mar. 1817, with bpts. in **OPR KLN** for Flory 1818, Mary 1820, Grace 1822, Patrick (q.v.) 1824. Other ch. in GK. In **CEN KLN** 1841 he is 40, with Mary 30, Mary 20, 'Petter' 16, Hector 12, Grace 18, but is not in 1851 census when his sons Peter (= Patrick) & Archibald are bachelors of 25 and 23. See his s. Archibald McLean who d. aged 33 at Penmore, 1860. Another Penmore boatman, Hugh McLean, 5 years older, may be a cousin. His w. Mary was dau. of Archie McLucais & Mairon McNeill.

MacLaine, Charles (1793-c.1835?) m. **Mary McMillan** and is in **GRO/LMD/Souls** of 1829 at Fishnish, aged 36 with 'Mrs Maclaine' 28, Mrs MacMillan [his mo.-in-law, or gr.-mo.-in law?] 76, Meron Maclaine 7, Donald Maclaine 5, Jessy Maclaine 1. He is absent from **CEN 1841** census perhaps dec., and Mary is a cottar aged 60 with her dau. Janet 10, [bpt. 16 Nov.1828], Catherine 8 and 'Marry' 4. The name is spelt MacLaine by LMD who wrote it this way for all the MacLaines in his **Souls**, but census has 'McLean'.

McLean, Charles (c.1795) m. **Mary McPhail** <1847; lived in Ledirkle, near present-day Fishnish. In **CEN TRS 1851** he is 55, cotton weaver, b. Gribun with Mary w. 39 b. TRS, Ann 3 & Marion McLean 'relation', wid. 83 b. Gribun. Mary McPhail d. at Ledirkle 31 Oct. 1860 aged 50, dau. of John McPhail farmer & Marion McDougall, and was bur. Pennygown. It appears Ann was an only ch. as **CEN TRS 1861** has Charles 'McLaine' wid. 65 wool weaver b. KLF [Gribun in KLF] & Anne 13 b. TRS. In 1881 the 'ane ewe lamb' has flown, and Charles is alone aged 75, a woollen weaver in 1 room.

McLean, Charles (c.1799-1887) crofter & wid. of **Mary McInnes** when he d. at Kinloch 20 Mar. 1887 aged 88. He was b. KLF s. of Murdoch McLean, weaver in Tiroran & Catherine McNeill whose only ch. in **KLF OPR** was Catherine, bpt. 9 May 1807, Charles's younger sister. Charles's dau., Margaret Stewart gave info at his death. His w. Mary had d. 9 Jan. 1882 aged 84, her f. being John McInnes, crofter, & her m. Sarah McLean. They had m. 3 Dec. 1827 when he was from Burg KLF, she from Lochbuy TRS. They moved from Tiroran to Balevulin and then to Kinloch, that dismal refuge for cottars dispossessed by landlords <1861. Ch. were Marion 1829, Catherine 1832, Peggy c.1834, Sandy c.1836 or later (who became a sailor). Peggy (Maggie) m. a Stewart, and was a wid. in Kinloch in 1881.

Maclean, Charles (1806-1872) s. of Donald Maclean WS (1770-1853) & Lillias Grant, he is spoken of frequently in his f.'s many letters in **NAS GD174/1628**. As a result of contracting ophthalmia at school in England, he was almost totally blind, but a man of great spirit and self-sufficiency, he put himself through university and Divinity School, but turned down by C. of S. on account of his blindness. After emotional upheavals such as his love for Jane Jarvis Maclaine (q.v.) of Lochbuy, he arranged to go to Canada in defiance of his f. His *credo* is set forth in a moving letter of 2 May 1834 to his bro-in-law, Murdoch Maclaine of LB: "*I sail for New York from Greenock in the LADY OF THE LAKE on Saturday... for the sake of being independent and having a house of my own, though it should only be a LOG one... I expect to have 400 sovereigns when I reach Upper Canada... and with that I must sink or swim for ever... My mind will often be in Mull where I have spent so many happy days.*" **NAS GD174/1688/3**. He revisited Scotland 1836-7 when he m. Murdoch's niece, **Jane Campbell**.

"Charles & his bride landed at Ardtornish from the Steamer... I understand the young wife left the Highlands in High Spirits. Poor thing – she little knows America or its hardships." Their 1st ch. was b. in Canada in 1838 when Jane's immature cousin John Campbell Maclaine (q.v.) wrote of the baby, *"Miss Lillian Maclean's nose is rather in the medium between Charles's and Jane's, as it is rather of the cock-up variety."* **NAS GD174/1714** Charles & Jane had 9 more ch., Donald, Jane, Colin, Jane Jarvis (after his lost love), William, Sibella, Archibald, Alexander & Charles. The blind Charles, through the deaths of a succession of bros., was to become representative of the Macleans of Drimnin, and the title passed from him to his s. Prof. Donald Maclean in Detroit. 4 of the ch. became doctors, and there must be many other Drimnin descendants in Canada and the USA. **JC/MIPGRO/Glouc**.

McLean, Charles (c.1808-1866) m. to **Ann McLean** he d. of bronchitis in Shore Street, TBR 1866 aged 58. His parents were Hector McLean feuar & Flora McNiven.

McLean, Charles (c.1810-1886) s. of a shepherd, Lachlan McLean & Sarah McGilvray, he was at Corrachy in **CEN 1841** aged 25, with Margaret 25, Margaret 5, Marion 3, John 1, and in **CEN 1851** at Rohill in Glenforsa as a shepherd in 1851 with 6 ch.. He gave info on death of his sister Mary McLaine (q.v.) at Torlochan Feb. 1856. He remained at Rohill until after 1871 when he was 60, but in 1781 his s. Dugald (q.v.) 28 also a shepherd w. a w. and 7 ch., had taken on the extended responsibility of Bentalla. Charles d. at Torlochan aged 76 in 1886 of inflammation of the lungs. His w. **Margaret McDougall** d. 10 Oct.1896, when her **CRD** said she was 90. Her parents were Dugald McDougall & Margaret McIntyre, but they came from Ardencaple (Kilbrandon), not Mull.

McLean, Charles (b.c. 1833)m. a girl from Uist, **Ann McPhail** in 1864, and their dau. Flora was b. KLF c.1866, another dau. Julian on 11 Mar. 1869. Charles was a quarrier at Camas, North Bay, KLF in **CEN KLF 1871**

Maclean, Charles Alexander Hugh (1874-1948) of Pennycross & Carsaig, 2nd s. of Archibald John of PX who 'parted with his estate' in 1888. C.A.H. Maclean m. in 1897 **Mabel Julia Maclaine** of LB, dau. of Murdoch Gillean Maclaine (q.v.)

McLean, Christina (1796-1873) w. of **Murdoch Maclaine** of LB. was b. Edinburgh and d. there 13 Feb.1873. In **CEN 1861** at Java Lodge, built for her by her s. Donald, aged 64, with unm. daus. Lillias 42, Jane 40, Elizabeth 36, Marianne 34 and 5 servants. In 'Java Village' was her head gardener William Henry 31, with his w. Alison 20 and s. William 3 mos.

McLean, Cirsty cottar's wid., she d. Balligown 1860 aged 84. Her f. was John McInnes, her mo. Margaret McLean. In **CEN KLN 1851** Balligown, Cursty McLean was head, m., pauper, b. KLN, with unm. dau. Mary 34 and Flory Mcfarlane gr.dau. 5 scholar, b. KLN.

McLean, Christina (1806-1892) wid. of **John McLaine or McLean** ploughman, she d. at Kingharair 1892 aged 79 [but bpt. at Sorn 1806], her parents being Neil McLean, farmer & Flora McLean. She had been confined to bed only 1 day, according to her s. Archibald McLaine. John & Chirsty were in ploughman's house at Kingharair in **CEN KLN 1851, '61, '71, '81**. John was b. at Raodle, and Cirsty at Sorne. They have a s. Hector b.c.1846 and dau. Mary c.1850, both at Kingharair. In 1861, John McLean [sic] is 55, ploughman, with Chirsty 48, Donald 21, 'scholars' Chirsty 15, Hector 13 & Mary 10, and Archy 8. There are no OPR bpts. for this family as they fall into GK years. <u>See</u> McLean, John (1802)

McLean, Christina (c.1817-1905) wid. of **Hugh McLean** carpenter, she d. at Ensay of old age in 1905 aged 88, when her parents' names were given as Kenneth McDougall farmer & Catherine McPhail. Info given by her nephew John McDougall.

McLean, Christina (c.1835-1891) dau. of John McLean herd & Sarah McRae, m. to **Norman McDonald** shepherd, she d. 8 Jun. 1891 of cancer at Ardura aged 56, her husb. present. Us.res. Scour KLF. **KLS CRD 1891**

McLaine, Christina (c. 1845-1884) m. to **James Cameron** shepherd she d. Garmony 16 Feb.1884 aged 39. Her parents were Donald McLaine & Ann McDonald; info from Duncan McLaine her bro. **TRS CRD**.

McLean, Christina d. 7 July 1857 aged 3 at Tostary, dau. of Coll McLean (q.v.) mason and Anne McLean, M/S McLean.

Maclaine, Colin Campbell 'child in fornication' nat. s. of Capt. Archibald Maclaine (q.v. *Sir Archibald Maclaine*) of 94th Regt. in Ledirkle & Mary Fletcher there. Bpt. 24 Aug.1806. So far nothing else is known of Colin. **TRS OPR**

McLean, Coll (1823-1854?) mason s. of George McLean & Christina McDonald; he m. 1853 Anne McLean dau. of Charles McLean & Mary Livingston and sister of Donald McLean in Tostary. He & Anne seem singularly unfortunate, with 3-year-old Christian dying of croup at Tostary 7 Jul. 1857 and 2-year-old Coll (reg. 1855 as Charles?) dying of scarlet fever in the same year. **Anne McLean** his w. d. at Langamull Jun. 1909 aged 84, w. of the late Coll McLean **GRV Kilninian**.

McLean, Coll (c.1860-1931) 'Colla Mor' ferryman for 52 yrs on Sound of Iona, s. of Allan McLean (q.v.) of the sloop Rosina & Jane McDonald. He m. Margaret McCormick who d. 19 Dec. 1926 aged 63. Colla Mor d. 21 May 1931 aged 71. **GRV Fionnphort**

Maclean, Donald (<1715-c.1770) mercht. in Glasgow, collector of customs at Montego Bay, he was a descendant of Hector Og and m. (1) **Mary Dickson**, mo. of Sir Hector Maclean (q.v.) 23rd of Duart who succeeded Sir Allan, 'the Knight' and (2) **Margaret Wall**, mo. of Sir Fitzroy Jeffreys Grafton Maclean (q.v.) 24th of Duart, ancestress of a line of Duart chiefs continuing to the present day.

Maclaine, Donald (c.1740-1820) 'Cousin Donald' to the Macquarie brothers, he was assistant to his uncle, Murdoch Maclaine (later of LB) in Edinburgh, looking after his business when MM was overseas. He became a seedsman in Anchor Close, Edinburgh, but kept links with Mull. He m. in 1772, but his w's name is uncertain, and they were childless. *"I was at your cousin Old Donald's funeral yesterday. He has left everything to his niece Flora … £600 to his nephew Forsyth & £12 a year to Flora's mother & £12 to Forsyth's. His fortune is very trifling. I very much suspect if Flora has £3,000 free it is the utmost… He has acted very unhandsomely… a raskally attempt to cheat you after his death…"* **NAS GD174/1628/194 JC/MIP**

Maclean, Donald (d.1748) 5th of Torloisk, fought at Sheriffmuir; a man of culture he m. **Mary Campbell** poss. c.1716, and had Hector (q.v.) his heir, Lachlan (q.v.), Allan (q.v. 1725-1797) the distinguished military man, Archibald (q.v.), Mary (unm. – protected by her bro. Allan), Anne (m. Donald McLean q.v. of Raodle), Alice (q.v. – m. Lachlan MacQuarrie of Ulva), Christian (m. Rev.Alexander McLean q.v. of Kilninian), Betty (unm.), Elizabeth (m. Lachlan Maclaine of Garmony and after his death James Park, Jamaica). For Donald Torloisk's funeral in 1748,

over a dozen sheep were slain, 6 casks of aquavit ordered from Calgary, over 23 lbs of cheese and 62 stones of meal consumed.

McLean, Donald (c.1760-1825) s. of Hector McLean (q.v.) of Killean, tacksman of Ardfenaig & Janet McLean; served in Penobscot, Maine 1779-83. Settled in Canada.

McLean, Donald (<1760) of Raodle, conspicuously absent from practical records, but mentioned by Maclean historians as 'the strong man of Raodle' he m. **Anne**, dau. of Donald **Maclean** (q.v.) of Torloisk. His s. George d. unm. but Hector McLean (q.v. – c.1770) was to m. Helen Campbell and become tacksman of Ensay & Mingary. A dau. Marion, m. Hugh McLean (q.v.) Ardchrishnish – later of Rossall and had a 'swarm' of hungry ch. Donald McLean himself remains obscured by his image as the strongest man in Mull.

Maclaine, Dr Donald (c.1766-1834) surgeon, bro. of Dr Andrew Maclaine (q.v.) he m. 21 Sep. 1791 **Mary McNicol**, dau. of Rev. Donald McNicol min. of Lismore, – *"a very fine woman"*. Their 16 ch. are listed at beginning of **TRS OPR**. He was wrongly accused of cuckolding Allan Maclaine (q.v.) of Scallastle. Family lived at Callachilly, where his house was coveted by Lachlan Macquarie later of NSW, then moved to Gualachaoilish TRS in 1829. Only the eldest dau. Anne Maclaine, is known to have had descendants. She m. the Rev. Alexander Kennedy, missionary at Salen & Tobermory, later min. of Jura, with 9 ch. Anecdotes of Dr Donald are told in **JC/MIP** His letters to MM are in **NAS.GD174/1454**. He d. Gualachaoilish 1834, bur. Pennygown Wed. 12 Feb. 1834. His ch. seemed to have reverted to the spelling Maclean, but there were possibly no 2nd generation descendants of the name.

McLean, Donald (<1765) more interesting for his absence from Mull than his presence there, he m. **Giles or Julian McArthur** 8 Jan. 1794 when he was at Kengharair and had 8 ch. at Arivelchyne and Balligown- Ann 1795; Hugh 1796; Hector 1899; John 1800; Christian 1802; Roderick 1803; Mary 1805; Isobel 1807. The mystery is in the fact that **LMD** in 1826 mentions he was *"assisted by James McLean, youngest s. of Donald McLean and Julian McArthur from Glasgow, now at Fanmore"* and there are further references to *"my servant man James McLean".* James not being in the list suggests the whole family went to Glasgow >1807, but that there were still relations in Fanmore (next to Balligown) for James to return to.

McLean, Donald (b.c.1767) cottar in Tavool, KLF he m. 28 Mar. 1809 **Catherine McKinnon** there, and is in **CEN KLF 1851** at Kinlochscridain aged 84, a small tenant with 8 acres b. TRS with Catherine 65, John 43, Allan 41, Lachlan 30, Marion 28 and Catherine 26, all b. Rossal & Kinloch.

McLean, Donald (<1770) after his marr. to **Isobel McNiven** on 31 Jan. 1792 when he was from Arin, he is head of a remarkably cohesive family of 10 ch. who seem to disappear from records after 1812. They are at Arin, Ensay (Argyll) and Balligown (Torloisk estate). Bpts in **KLN OPR** are of John 1792; Ann 1794; Lauchlan 1796; Hugh 1798; Mary 1800; Flora 1803; Archibald 1805; Janet 1807; Catherine 1810; Duncan 1812.

McLean, Donald (<1770) like Donald above, this man, who m. **Mary Campbell** 20 Mar. 1792 had an orderly family before disappearing from Arin, KLN c.1814. Bpts. in **KLN OPR** are of Mary 17 Dec. 1792, Donald 1794, Catherine 1798, John 1803 [after a gap when Donald, a fencible soldier, was away for a few years?] Donald 1804, Donald 1806, Janet 1809, Grace 1812, Alexander 1813.

McLean, Donald (1770-1861) tenant in Iona m. to **Flora McFee** or McPhee <beginning of OPR. Their ch. in **KLF OPR** were Cirsty 1805, Lachlan 1807, Ann 1809, Hector 1811, Mary 1813, Catherine 1816. In **CEN KLF Iona 1841**, Donald was 70 and Flora 60, with Hector 25 and Mary 20, ages rather far out. In 1861 at Sligeanach, Iona, Hector has become 96 and Flora 86, and their s. Hector is running the farm even if Donald is nominal head. Donald's death on 16 Jul. 1861 confirms his age on death as 97, and his parents' names are given as Hector McLean and Catherine McDonald. His f. Hector is in fact in Iona in **ERC/Inhabitants 1779** aged 40, when Donald himself is 9. Flora McFee, absent from Iona in **CEN KLF 1851** is to be discovered staying with her wid. dau. Mary McLean, 35, at Scour KLF, and 3 gr.ch. See McLean, Mary (b.1813) Flora d. 18 Nov. 1862 in Iona. Her parents were John McFee or McPhie and Catherine Cameron. This family is one of the few with continuity right through from the Duke's census (**ERC/Inhabitants**) to the recent past, for Sligeanach remained in the hands of descendants until the death of Hector Maclean in 1956.

McLean, Donald, WS (1770-1853) s. by 2nd marr. of Allan McLean (q.v.) of Drimnin to Mally Maclaine of LB. Donald was b. in Edinburgh and apprenticed to the lawyer Colquhoun Grant, whose dau. **Lillias Grant** he m. in 1793. There were 16 ch., the oldest dau., Christina m. young Murdoch Maclaine (q.v.) of LB. Another dau. Sibella (q.v.) m. Alexander Crawford. Donald was involved in legal work for most of the landowners in Mull between 1895 and 1840. He had 16 ch., but as his family tree, his life and personality are all recorded in **JC/MIP** they need not be described here.

McLean, Donald (<1775) an unusually shapely record for the family of Donald & his w. **Mary Lamont** in Cuilinish KLN gives no clue about their disappearance >1817, but we know that times were hard at that point, and they would have done well to emigrate. Their marr. was 24 Apr. 1798, followed by Alexander in Apr. 1799, Catherine 1801, John 1803, Ann 1805, Elizabeth 1808, Mary 1810, Flora 1812, Margaret 1814, Allan 1817.

McLean, Donald (<1780) This Donald m. **Mary Morrison** <1801 when Mary his dau. was bpt. in Fanmore KLN, then in Kilbrenan 9 more ch. were bpt. – Marion 1804, Euphemia 1806, Anne 1807, Archy 1809, Catherine 1811, John 1813, Hector ? 1815, Neil 1817, Janet 1820. In **CEN KLN 1841** at Kilbrenan Donald is 65, Mary 53, young Mary 35, Catherine 25, John 23, Neil 21, Janet 20. Donald is 75 in 1851 with young Mary 45, Jessy [Janet] 30 and a grandson called Andrew Stevenson 12. See McLean, Janet (1820-1905).

McLean, Donald (c.1785) crofter in Ardchiavaig or Uisken KLF, he m. **Catherine McLucais** in Suie KLF 20 Jun. 1824. **KLF OPR** has bpts. for Catherine 1825, Hugh 1827, Flora 1829, Isabella 1831, Alexander 1835, Archibald 1837, Charles 1840. In **CEN KLF 1841**, with Donald 55, Catherine 45, a John of 22 appears, a nat. ch. or a s. from a former marr.? Otherwise all the ch. have survived, with a Sarah added in c. 1833. In 1851 at Uisken, Donald 71 & Catherine 54 have only Alexander 14 and Archibald 12 'scholars.'

McLean, Donald (b.1786) m. as a crofter in Creich, KLF, **Janet McCallum** also Creich on 22 Jun.1809. Neil was bpt. 1 Nov. 1810, John 6 Sep. 1812, Allan 20 Nov. 1814, Hector 29 Jun. 1817, Janet 10 Nov. 1819, Marion 12 May 1822, Alexander 2 Sep. 1824, Flora 29 Oct. 1826, Mary 2 Jul. 1829. **KLF OPR** & last one **ION QS OPR**. There were 2 Donald McLeans who were crofters in Creich at this time, one d. 11 Feb. 1837, but D. Whyte's *Dictionary of Scottish Emigrants to Canada* claims that this Donald & Janet with 9 ch. went to Lochaber, Ottawa County in 1829, and other descendants of Donald and Janet have emerged in N. America who have evidence of Janet being the dau. of Alexander McCallum and Catherine McGillivray. In the absence of earlier **KLF OPR**s, this seems acceptable.

McLean, Donald m. to Mary Currie; <u>see</u> McLean, Mary (c.1781-1861)

McLean, Donald (c.1787-1867) mercht. s. of Donald McLean farmer & Peggy McLean, M/S McLean, he d. 8 Nov.1867 aged 80 in Tobermory when his s. Alexander gave info.

McLean, Donald (<1790) m. **Margaret McLean** <1810 and had in **KLN OPR** in Kilbrenan/Balligown area of Torloisk estate: Flora 1810, John 1812, Lachlan 1814, Mary 1815, John 1818, Ann 1820, Donald 1822, Alexander 1824. A Margaret McLean in Balligown in **CEN KLN 1841** aged 44 with Alexander 15 may be the remnant of this family, but Balligown is full of McLean widows. The laird of Torloisk had rightly boasted that everyone on his estate was a McLean.

McLean, Donald (c.1792-1837) crofter in Creich who m. **Ann McArthur** in Caitchean (she d.1880, aged 88) on 23 Feb. 1815. Bpts. in **KLF OPR**: Isabella 1816, Alexander 1817, Marion 1819, Mary 1822, Dugald 1824, twins Donald & Janet 1826, another Dugald 1829 and Isabella 1832. In **ION OPR 1837** Donald's death is reported on 11 Feb. 1837. In **CEN KLF 1841** the family is in Catchean Wintertown where 'Widow' McLean is 40, Donald & Jess the twins are 12, Dugald is 10, Isobel 8 and Neil 5. In **CEN KLF 1851** at Drimcruaidhcroft, Ann's s. Donald, said to be 21, is head of a household consisting of bro. Dugald 19, sister Flora 22, sister Bell 17, bro. Neil 15 and his mo. Ann McArthur 58. Donald Junior (q.v.) was to m.Christina Black and d. at Kentra in 1902, when his true age was given as 76.

Maclaine, Donald (c.1793-1855) m. to **Ann McDonald** he was b. Ledirkle TRS s. of Charles McLean shepherd & Cirsty Black; had been in district all his life when he d. 24 Mar. 1855 at Ledirkle aged 62. His ch. were 1. John 18, 2. Allan 16, 3. Charles 14, 4. Gillean 12, 5. Chirsty 10, 6. Duncan 6, 7. Ann 3. Bur. Pennygown. Info. Murdoch McLean (q.v.) X bro. Reg. Lochdonhead 28 Mar. 1855. His name is spelt Maclaine in OPR and elsewhere, but <u>McLean</u> in **CEN TRS 1851** at Ledirkle, when he is 55, shepherd, b. TRS , with Ann 39, b. MRV; Allan 14, Gillean 10 & Christina 6 all 'scholars'; Duncan s. 1 and Janet McLean, relation unm. 45. His marr. to Anne McDonald, Ardnadrochit was 4 Jul. 1833. In **LMD/Souls** at Ledirkle, 1829, Donald, still unm. 36 is living with both parents and with Murdoch Maclaine (*q.v. under McLean*) his bro., and Janet Maclaine 20. <u>See</u> ref. to Ledirkle tenants in **JC/MIP** p. 283.

McLean, Donald (>1793<1806-d.1897) b. Knapdale, Argyll, but age wavers through records. About 1833 he m. **Margaret Dewar** dau. of Rev. Hugh Dewar & Mary Brisette Campbell, moved to Bunessan where he was accorded the title 'Mr' in OPR and was in **CEN KLF 1841** at Bunessan as postmaster aged 34 with w. 32, Mary Brisette 5, Elizabeth 3, Susan Jane 1. Other ch. b. KLF were George Duncan b. 5 Dec. 1834, Hugh b.1843, Emily & Maggie. He was also a grocer in Bunessan, and involved in aid operations in 1840s when potato famine struck. He moved out of Bunessan Village to Cnocknacaroch, nr. Taoslin. His w. Margaret d. on Christmas Eve 1892 aged 91 at Salen when her s.-in-law John McKenzie gave info. Donald, living to a ripe old age, went on the Poor Roll and d. at Fionnphort 6 Aug. 1897 aged 104 according to Alexander McGregor, Insp. of Poor, who gave Donald's parents' names as Hugh McLean, stone quarrier & Mary McTaggart. He had suffered 'senile decay' 3 yrs.

McLean, Donald (c.1794-1885) shoemaker in Knocknafenaig KLF he m. **Marion Beaton** in Ardchiavaig 23 Apr. 1818, but absence of infant bpts in **KLF OPR** suggest Baptist leanings, his area being the centre of what mins. described as 'Anabaptist error'. In **CEN KLF 1841** he is 40, with Marion 40, Neil 14, Elizabeth 12, Archibald 9, Malcolm 7 and Margaret 5. In **CEN KLF 1851**, still at Knocknafenaig, he is 56, Marion 57, Neil 24, Malcolm 17, and Margaret 15.Most of this family went to Canada shortly after this census, settling in Saugeen Township, Ontario, where Donald and Marion (or Sarah) and their s. Malcolm are buried (Port Elgin).

McLean, Donald (c.1794-1874) gardener b. Ardnacross KLN s. of Hector McLean crofter & Jane Campbell, m. 1844 at Druimfin to **Mary McLean**, he d. 7 Oct. 1874 at Dervaig aged 80 of 'infirmities of old age' being confined to bed only 1 day; a relative, Helen Campbell, gave info. A DM is in **CEN KLN 1871**, Dervaig aged 70, retired gardener. He has a w. Mary 50, laundress b.

MULL
PLACENAMES
MENTIONED
IN THE TEXT

Tay
Tobermory
Ledaig
liscate
Druimfin

ISA

termore

Ardnacross

Arle

Tenga

Aros Castle

Achadashenaig

Kellan
Killiechronan
Salen
Ledirkle

emore
Corrynachenchy
Fishnish
Balmeanach

GLEN FORSA

Rhoail

Knock
Scallastle

LOCH BA
Bradil
Craignure

GLEN CANNEL
Coiregairn

Duart

Achnacroish

Torness
Kilpatrick
Ardchoirk
Gorten

Ardachoil
Gleannan

Dererach
Grass Point

Ardura
Auchnacraig

inloch
Rossal
Fellonmore
Killean

Pennyghael
BROLASS
Kinlochspelve
Druimaain
Croggan

naig
Dalnaha
Portfield

Lochbuie
Moy
Barrachandroman

Glenbyre

Laggan

Carsaig
Glenlibidil

KLN and s. Hector 16 'scholar'. In **CEN KLN 1851** this family was at Druimfin with Donald McLean **Mason** being 55, Mary McLean w. 30, Sarah dau. 6; Janet dau.4, Anne dau. 1. This is not inconsistent. The Macleans of Coll owned both Dervaig & Druimfin and would have moved employees.

McLean, Donald (c.1794-1855) s. of Charles Maclaine (q.v.) shepherd & Chirsty Campbell, he was b. Ledirkle TRS, nr. present-day Fishnish, and m. there on 4 Jul. 1833 **Anne McDonald**, b. MRV, in Ardnadrochit TRS. He was in **GRO/Glouc./LMD/Souls** in 1829 with his parents Charles 57 and Chirsty 54 at Ledirkle, when Donald was 36 and his bro. Murdoch 32. The family is referred to in **GRO/LMD**, being near neighbours of the diarist. Donald d. 24 Mar.1855 aged 62, when his ch. were John (18 in 1855), Allan (16 in 1855), Charles (14 in 1855), Gillean (12 in 1855), Chirsty (10 in 1855), Duncan (6 in 1855), Anne 3 at her f.'s death. These correspond with **CEN TRS 1851**. He had never left Ledirkle, and his bro. Murdoch who supplied details at his death gave his mo.'s name as Campbell where **TRS OPR** has Black, and Murdoch's own CRD has Black.

McLean, Donald (c.1800) crofter in Dervaig b. in Mingary, he m. a **Mary** from Penmore poss. c.1830, so all baptisms are lost in GK. Ch. reconstructed from censuses are: Catherine, Hugh, Allan, John, Neil, Flora, Donald, Mary, b. between 1833-1852. He can be confused with the gardener Donald McLean above.

Maclaine, Donald (c.1805-1850s ?) shoemaker b. TRS m. **Jean or Jane McLean** (q.v. – who as his wid. d. Oskamull KLN 22 Mar. 1874 aged 60, dau. of Charles McLean crofter & Christina Cameron). In **CEN KLN 1841** Donald was 45, with Jean 34 at Corkamull KLN with Margaret 10, Allan 8, Ann 6, John 3, Cirsty 1; in **CEN KLN 1851** Donald is only 48, with Jean 40, John 13 & Mary 8 both b. SLN; Jane 6 & Charles 2 were b. ULV which means Corkamull, not the island. Donald must have d. before 1855. By 1861 Jean at 53 has a McNeill gr.-s. Donald 5. A Peggy McLean, wid., 82 attached to household may be the dec. Donald's mo. By 1871 Jean is 64, supported by her family, Allan 38, Ann 35, Charles 21 and Donald 15. Jean was also b. TRS.

McLaine, Donald (<1805) boatman in Ledirkle, nr. present-day Fishnish, aged 35 in **CEN TRS 1841** with his w. **Mary** [**McEachern**] 25,

Catherine 8, Hector 6, Duncan 4, Neil 2. Duncan & Neil's bpts. can be found in **TRS** OPR in 1837 and 1839. There is also a Janet bpt. in 1843. No sign of the family in 1851 in Ledirkle, Fishnish or Salen.

McLean, Donald (1807-1877) miller, s. of Hugh McLean (q.v.) miller and Flora Morrison. He m. **Mary McLean** in Feb. 1842, had Hugh 1843-1917 (also a miller), Flora 1844, Hector 1847, twins Charles & Mary 1850, Catherine 1852-1910, Alexander 1854-1942, Grace 1856 & Ann 1859. Donald d. at Kellan aged 68, 1877. Mary McLean, dau. of Charles McLean the Penmore boatman & Mary McLucaish, d. in Salen 1897.

McLean, Donald (bpt. 1814 d. 1871) 1 of 3 bros. who owned Gometra. See McLean, Hector (1772-1846) his f.

McLean, Donald MD (b.1815) bpt. 27 Sep. 1815 s. of the Rev. Neil Maclean, min. of Tiree (who was s. of Donald Maclean, min. of the Small Isles) and his w. Isabella Macdonald, youngest dau. of Major Alexander Macdonald of Vallay, North Uist. He m. an **Anne** and in **CEN 1841** Calgary, Donald Maclean, Surgeon, 25, and Anne, with his sisters Lilly & Isabella happen to be staying overnight at Calgary on the night of the census. He took the farm of Kinlochspelvie in 1844 and was called in to attend Murdoch Maclaine 20th of LB on the night he d., in August 1844. There is correspondence concerning Donald in **NAS GD174/1181** and **1978**.

McLean, Donald (c.1816) m. in 1854 at Langamull to **Isabella McDonald**, they are in **CEN 1881 KLN** next to Bellachroy Inn, Dervaig with James 19, a rural letter-carrier (he was b. 1 Aug. 1861 at Dervaig), Neil 17, lab., Ann 14, Isabella 11, John 9, Maggie 9 and Catherine 6. **CEN 1871** has a Mary 17 and a Malcolm 13 older than James, at Cuin Farm, Dervaig, and all b. KLN. Isabella McDonald was b. Aintuim.

Maclaine, Donald (1816-1863) of Lochbuy 'Dod' 2nd s. of Murdoch 20th of LB & Christina Maclean, dau. of Donald Maclean WS (q.v.). Said to have been *wonderfully attentive* as a schoolboy. He went to Java to make his fortune with his distant cousin Gillean Maclaine (q.v.) gr.s. of Gillean of Scallastle (q.v.) exporting coffee. "*I am as happy as the day is long here, in town all day making money and in the country all the evening making love*" [1839]. He had fallen in love with Gillean's young Dutch sister-in-law, who left Java 1840 with Gillean, his w., another sister & their mo. to visit Britain, and all perished on the voyage. 'Dod', following in another ship, was not to learn of the tragedy until he arrived in Britain. Crushed by this event, he suffered a nervous breakdown, but returned to Batavia and m. there **Emilie Guillamine Vincent**, dau. of a Dutch businessman in 1844. Their s. Murdoch Gillean Maclaine (q.v.) was b. in Java in 1845. In his absence, his f. Murdoch d. 1844, his bro. Murdoch inherited an estate encumbered with debt, LB was sequestrated, and his bro. d. 1850. Donald set about the task of paying his bro.'s and f.'s debts, de-entailing LB, removing encumbrances, then buying estate back at £31,000 with his own funds. Returning to Mull in 1854, he settled his family at LB, spent 8 years restoring the property, building Java Lodge for his mo. & sisters, before his premature death in Edinburgh 12 Oct. 1863. The estate went to his s. Murdoch Gillean (q.v.) with a portion to Anthony Vincent Maclaine (1846-1887) his 2nd s. There were 3 daus. Emilie, who m. Frederick Campbell of the Airds family, Rosa, and Christian. **JC/MIP**

McLaine, Donald (1817-1870) bpt. at Moy 23 Mar. 1817 s. of John McLaine and Catherine Livingston, he d. at Crogan aged 53 on 20 Mar. 1870 of a liver complaint, his bro. John McLaine supplying info. His w. **Catherine Livingston** (who had the same maiden name as his mo.) had been previously m. to Dugald Currie, an elder in Kinlochspelve Kirk. His mo. Catherine Livingston was still alive aged 80 at the time of his death. **TRS OPR,CRD KLS, CEN TRS**.

McLean, Donald (1819) subtenant in Torloisk, he m. a girl from Barra, **Catherine McNeill** (known as 'Ketty') 27 Nov. 1855 in Ulva parish.She d. 1905 aged 79. Donald McLean was s. of George McLean and his first w. Christina McDonald, and was bpt. at Cragaig, Ulva 15 Aug. 1819. In **CEN KLN 1851** at Burg, Donald is unm. 31 living with his f. George McLean 60, step-mo. Sarah McNeill 35, his bro. John 23, and sister Chirsty 17. In 1861 at Burg, Donald, 40, is m. to Ketty McNeill with ch. Chirsty 5, George 3, Sally 1, all b. KLN with James McNeil, servant, 18, ploughman, b. Barra. In **CEN KLN 1881** DM 61, crofter, with Catherine 52, George unm. 22, Coll s. unm. 19; Catherine dau. 16.

McLaine, Donald (<1818) m. to Ann McDonald. See McLaine, Christina his dau. (c.1845-1884) **TRS CRD**

McLean, Donald (1826-1902) ag.lab. in Kintra

KLF, s. [1 of twins] of Donald McLean (q.v.) crofter and Ann McArthur. He was in Catchean Wintertown in **CEN KLF 1841** with wid. mo. & siblings, and in **CEN KLF 1851** still in this family group aged 21 with bro. Dugald 19, sister Flora 22, sister Bell 17, bro. Neil 15 & Ann his mo. 58. In **CEN KLF 1861** Donald was already a wid. at 38 with Jane 16, Anne 14, Catherine 11, Donald 9, Hector 7, Dugald 5. In **CEN KLF 1881** he was left with Donald 18 & Dugald 14. Donald's mo. Ann who had lived with her unm. s. Neil, a granite quarrier in Kintra, d. aged 88 in 1880. Donald d. aged 76 of cancer of the leg, in 1902, wid. of **Christina Black**.

Maclean, Donald (c.1833-1910) s. of Charles Maclean (q.v.) & Mary Livingston, m. to Sarah Maclean, he d. 2 Dec. 1910 at Langamull aged 77 of bronchitis and old age. Allan Maclean his s. was present.

McLean, Donald (c.1874-1887) d. Kinloch KLF of scarlet fever aged 13, 11 Mar. 1887, s. of Lachlan McLean (q.v.) rural post runner & Catherine McGilvray. C. McLean, his mo. giving info. His 11 year-old sister d. 2 days later.

McLean, Captain Dugald (c.1762-1818) s. of Hector McLean (q.v.) & Janet McLean, he m. **Susanna** (1768-1847) dau. of the Rev. Neil **Macleod** & Margaret McLean, on 14 Feb. 1804. There were 5 ch., Mary Flora 1805, Janet Catherine 1807, Susanna 1808, Hector Neil 1811, Donald William 1814. He was drowned near Crinan in 1818.

McLean, Dugald (b.1841) s. of Charles McLean (sometimes spelt McLaine) (q.v.) and Margaret McDougall, his mo. coming from Kilbrandon parish. He m. **Chirsty McPhail**, dau. of John McPhail & Ann Campbell, in Oban 1869. In 1881 he was 37, shepherd at Bentalla, on the Glenforsa estate, with 7 ch.

McLean, Duncan (<1755) of Uisken; s. of John Maclaine or McLean, who was bur. at Knock at an unknown date and re-interred at Iona by contrivance of his s. Col. Alexander McLean (q.v.) Duncan m. **Mary Maclaine**; their ch. were Alexander (q.v.) 1777, John, Catherine (q.v. 1785-1875) Marion, Janet (q.v. 1789-1869), Archibald Lieut. 56th Regt., Duncan Lieut. 56th Regt., Elizabeth d. 1815.

McLean, Duncan (<1790) crofter in Creich; m. 24 Jan. 1811 Mary McArthur; ch. in **KLF & ION OPRs**: Mary 1812, Ann 1814, Marion 1816, John

1818, James 1821, Ann 1823, Dugald 1826, Margaret 1830. Although a large family, the individuals have proved untraceable, and the most unusual name, James, does not have a convincing re-appearance.

McLean, Lieut. Duncan (<1790) s. of Duncan McLean of Uisken, younger bro. of Lt.-Col. Alexander McLean of Uisken, he served in 56th Regt., and after the French wars returned to KLF, where his 2 nat. sons, John and Gillean, were b. to Margaret McDonald in 1824 and 1827;no trace of the sons in **CEN KLF 1841**, but some possible descendants are known to the author.

McLean, Duncan (c.1790) in Kinloch when he m. 9 Mar. 1824 **Catherine Boyd** in Siaba; ch. bpt. in Siaba: Angus 1825, Margaret 1827, Hector 1830, Una 1835. In **CEN KLF 1841** Duncan 'McLaine' 50 with Catherine 35, Angus 15, Margaret 14, Hector 11, Anne 4, Duncan 6 mo. This may be the Duncan of Lovat Cemetery, Bruce Township, Ontario who d. aged 88, a native of Mull.

Maclean, Rev. Duncan (1796-1871) min. of Salen 1828-1835, he was b. at Killin, Perthshire, s. of Archibald Maclean, cabinet maker. He m. 1828 **Flora Macleod**, dau. of Kenneth M., tacksman of Ebost. He joined the FC after working in Salen, Kilbrandon and Glenorchy. He was a close friend of LMD who enjoyed his erudition. His ch. were Murdoch Donald & Flora b. Salen 1829 and 1830, then Archibald, Margaret, Sarah, Kenneth, Anne Shaw & John Teed. He wrote poetry, and contributed Gaelic songs to periodicals.

McLean, Duncan (c.1799-1866) s. of Allan McLean & Ann McLean, he also m. an **Ann McLean** c.1832 in KLN, so baptism of his s. 'Lachlan Post' (q.v. McLean, Lachlan c.1833-1892), at Fanmore, is lost in GK. In **CEN KLN 1851** at Fanmore, KLN Duncan 52, Ann 46, Lachlan 17, Ann 12, Jessy 8, Allan 5 – but they migrated to Kinloch, KLF in 1850s where Duncan was a tenant 68, in **CEN KLF 1861** with Ann 65, Lachlan 25 a 'scholar', Janet 17, Allan 12. Duncan d. 31 Aug. 1866 at Kinloch, when Lachlan Post was present. Ann McLean d. at Kinloch 28 Dec. 1888 aged 87 of 'general decay'. She was dau. of Lachlan McLean crofter & Catherine McLean, M/S McLean.

McLean, Duncan (bpt.1801) in the hamlet of Acharn in 1861, this Duncan had a 9-year-old s. William McLean, a great help in identifying him. Due to the GK, there is no marr. for Duncan,

whose w. **Ann McDonald** had been b. in Glasgow, and had been m. before, with 2 daus. But the plot in Acharn thickens, for in **CEN KLN 1841** in a cottage in Acharn there dwelt a wid. Margaret McDonald 50, with wid. Ann McDonald 25, a Flora McDonald 6, Donald McDonald 4, Janet McDonald 1. On 6 May 1844 a nat. son was bpt. to Duncan McLean & Ann McDonald. In **CEN KLN 1851** Duncan 40 & Ann 35 are m. with little Duncan 7, Effy 5 and Flora & Janet, the 2 step-daus. Duncan's mother Catherine 80 is with this family, as is Duncan's bro. Donald McLean 38. The evidence points to Duncan being the s. of Lachlan & Catherine McLean in Acharn.

Maclean, Duncan (c.1810) m. **Ann McDonald** after a nat. s. Duncan had been bpt. at Acharn, 6 May 1844. In **CEN KLN 1851** at Acharn, Duncan is 40, Ann McDonald 35, Duncan 7, Effy 5, Flora McDonald step-dau. 18, Janet McDonald step-dau. 12. Duncan's mo. Catherine McLean, wid., 80, & his bro. Donald unm. 38 are with them. He was more likely to have been bpt. in 1801, as his parents were prob. Lachlan McLean (q.v. b.c.1774) & Catherine McLean.

McLaine, Duncan (bpt.1816) s. of Charles McLaine and Catherine McLaine (c.1785-1864) in Tobermory.

McLean, Duncan (c.1817-1867) pauper, wid., s. of Neil McLean & Chirsty McLean, he d. at Tobermory 20 Dec. 1867 aged 50.

McLean, Duncan (c.1823-1907) crofter m. to **Ann McFarlane**, he d. of 'senile decay' at Achnahaird, Ardtun 23 Jul. 1907 aged 84. His parents were Neil McLean, crofter & Flora McLean M/S McFarlane. His s. Archibald Maclean was present.

McLean, Elizabeth (<1790-1815) dau. of Duncan McLean of Uisken, she was prob. b.<1790, as she m. in 1806 **John McLean** in Scour. The couple lived in Suie, and had John (1811), Ann (1813), Allan (1814) and Archibald (1815) bpt. in KLF OPR, but Elizabeth had d.before the last bpts. A Margaret Maclean who m. Neil McCallum, boat builder in Ardtun was also a dau., and one of the relatives who contested the will of her uncle Lieut-Col. Alexander McLean (1777-1859).

Maclaine, Elizabeth (1790-1837) 'Eliza' dau. of Murdoch Maclaine of LB and Jane Campbell. She m., 2 Mar. 1820 in spite of family opposition to the match, **Donald Campbell** (1785-1841) s. of the 'Old Fox', Alexander Campbell, tacksman of Achnacraig. Their ch. were Jane (1820), Alexander (1821), Murdoch (1822), Anne Jean (1824), Catherine Janice (1825) and Elizabeth Henrietta (1827). Her husb. considered going to Jamaica in 1827 "*I am forced to banish myself*". In 1830 he was in serious debt, and friends said, "*he has cleverness and knowledge if he could guide his own actions... the improvident extravagant deeds of insanity ... gets into a violent passion if I find fault... when drinking he would give his name for £1,000 to any man...* After death of his w. he lived at Carsaig and d. May 1841. Of his ch. Murdoch & Catherine Janice d. 1834 and 1826. The other poor orphans were in the care of their uncle Ronald Campbell, and a long correspondence about their patrimony is in **NAS GD174/1724/8**

McLean, Elizabeth (c.1804?-1890) housekeeper, single, dau. of John McLean (q.v.) schoolmaster & Margaret McCallum, she d. at Maclean Land, TBR aged 83. She is not in list of 8 ch. bpt. to these parents, or in any census with them.

McLean, Elizabeth (c.1809-1874) m. to Alexander Livingston farmer she d. 18 Dec. 1874 at Raodle, of a 'supposed cold' by which she was confined to bed 2 mo., aged 65, her s. Donald Livingstone being present; parents were Donald McLean crofter & Mary Lamont.

McLaine, Elizabeth (d.1856) dau. of Angus McLaine, farm lab., & Catherine McPhail (M/S McPherson), she d. 18 Jan. 1856, single, and with no age given at death.

Maclaine, Elizabeth Harriet (1824-1885) dau. of Murdoch Maclaine 20th of LB & Christina McLean, dau. of Donald McLean WS.She m. at Java Lodge, 12 Jul. 1864, **Dr John McKenzie**, then aged 35 (to her 40, although she gave her age, in true LB style, as 34), and d. at Tighnabruaich in 1885, apparently without ch. Her husb. m. again, but d. in 1889 as a result of an accident in Glasgow.

Maclaine, Emilia Frances (b.1796), nat. dau. of Allan Maclaine (q.v.) of Scallastle TRS and Mary Gillies she was bpt. 10 Mar. 1796, and brought up by a Mrs Scott, York Street, Glasgow, where LMD, her uncle, called to see her Sun. 7 May 1815 "*a pretty, modest lassie, and prudent*". She m. Donald Gillies (it is not known if he was related to her mo.) boatman in the customs service at Greenock 14 Jun. 1816 (when her name was spelt McLean); they had a s. Allan Gillies bpt. 12

Oct.1817, a dau. Isobel 3 Oct. 1819, a dau. Mary 15 Jun. 1823, all at Greenock Old Parish. Emilia must have d. after that. LMD described her husb. Donald as "*an industrious well-doing person, bringing up his eldest son Allan and indeed the whole of his family well.*" The Gillies family returned frequently to Mull from Greenock or Port Glasgow. On 3 May 1832 LMD wrote "*My young friend Allan Gillies from Port Glasgow...appears a fine smart boy and a good scholar. His stepmother he left with her sister at Salen and is to join her on Sunday as she proceeds for Ulva to see her mother and the rest of her family.*" And again on 20 Oct. 1832 LMD wrote "*Allan Gillies, A Emilia's son, came to see me today from Salen previous to his departure for home to Port Glasgow, whether he expects to accompany his stepmother and her children in a few days.*" Donald Gillies's 2nd w. was Sarah Currie, whose dau. another Mary Gillies, m. John McColl, baker in Greenock, Port Glasgow and TBR. This couple had a dau. Emilia McColl 6 in **CEN TBR 1861**. It would appear that Lachlan Gillies (d.1863) in Tobermory was related to Donald G., since he & his w. Mary Livingston (Baliochdrach) bpt. their dau. Emilia on 2 Jan. 1826. Also, an Allan Gillies in TBR m. Janet McKinnon, and might have been a bro. of Donald G. These 3 Gillieses, Donald, Lachlan & Allan, may be sons of Angus Gillies & Isabel McLean. in **CEN TBR 1851**, Allan 55 a ship's carpenter, has Janet 42 and Janet's bro. Walter McKinnon 37, joiner living with them. Allan d. >1851. In **CEN TBR 1861** Jessie (Janet) was a wid. living with other Gillieses. Emilia's husb. Donald d. aged 97 in Tobermory 15 Dec. 1875, more than half a century after his first w. Emilia's Allan continued to live in Port Glasgow. It is not known if he had descendants, but if so, an interesting offshoot from 'Lochbuy loins', as Hugh Kingairloch would have said, since Emilia was a gr. gr.dau. of John Maclaine of Lochbuy. For background see **JC/MIP**

McLean, Emily (c.1845) dau. of Donald McLean (d.1897) mercht. in Bunessan, and Margaret Dewar (d.1892).

Maclean, Euphemia (c.1816-1875) she d. of influenza as wid. of **Hugh Maclean**, mercht. in Iona 2 Jan. 1875 at the age of 59. Her parents were Lachlan Maclean, farmer & Catherine Maclean. Her husb. Hugh had d. in 1863.In **CEN KLF ION 1871** she was 58 and kept 'the SHOP' Iona. Hers. Lachlan Maclean and dau. Margaret were in Iona Cottage, next door. She and Hugh had been m. 14

Jun. 1836. There was a 3rd ch. Mary b.1851 who does not seem to have survived.

McLean, Euphemia (c.1846) gr.-dau. of Duncan MacPhail 72 and his w. Flora MacKinnon 60 in **CEN ION 1851** at Cuilbhuirg, she was b. in TRS. She was the dau. of Chirsty McPhail & Alexander McLean (q.v.) who emig. to Australia 1852-3.

Maclaine, Farquhar (1743-1822) 'Honest Farquhar' carpenter in Oskamull m. **Betty Macquarie**, sister of Lachlan Macquarie of NSW, 5 Jul. 1771 when he was in Laggan. Bpts: Mary 1772; Murdoch 1774; [unfinished entry, female – Ann] 1776; Hugh 1781; Hector 1783; Flora 1786; Margaret 1794. He had a joint tenancy of a farm in Oskamull with his mo.-in-law, Peggy Maclaine, sister of Murdoch Maclaine 19th of LB. In **CRG/Inhabitants 1779** he is shown as tenant of Achadashenaig, as Oskamull was under that farm, aged 36, with Murdoch, s., 5, his w., daus and mo.-in-law (4 unnamed females). He was employed by MM for the joinery work in Lochbuy House in 1788. His s. Hector was 'massacred' at Candia in 1803. "*Our friends at Oskamull have signalled nothing of their great loss, but the honest father suspects it much but behaves very prudently…needless to conceal the unhappy news any longer from them…*". His s. Murdoch (q.v.) was disturbed, serving at St Vincent in 1802, that his parents did not write. When Farquhar d. in 1822 he was "*as good and honest a man as ever spelt the name of Maclaine*" according to Governor Macquarie. Betty d. at Oskamull in 1833 aged about 85, and was bur. at Kilvickewen, Ulva, "*an elegant cold collation at the Colonel's [Charles Macquarie] house at Ardnacaillich*".

McLean, Farquhar (c.1760) In **CEN 1841** of Ardalanish FM is 80 and living alone, and may be the same FM who was in **ERC/Inhabitants 1779** aged 14 s. of Duncan McLean, keeper.

McLean, Farquhar (c.1778) m. **Catherine Fletcher** (c.1785-1855), Scallastlebeg. They had one s., John, who was dec. on his mo.'s death at Craignure in 1855.

McLean, Farquhar (18th C.) in **ERC/Inhabitants 1779** name of 3 males, (1) aged 12 at Potie KLF (2) aged 14 at Ardalanish KLF (3) aged 36 at Oskamull KLN. The last is 'honest Farquhar's s.-in-law of Peggy Macquarie or Maclaine. Of the first two, very close in age, there was one in Ardalanish in 1841 census aged 80 , living alone, with no w.'s name to identify him. One Farquhar McLean m. a Catherine McQuarrie.

McLaine, Farquhar (18th C.) crofter in Ardtun, KLF, m. **Catharine McQuarie** <1812. Only 1 s. in records.

McLean, Finlay (b.1791) s. of John McLean & Jean McDonald in Peinmollach KLN. His parents m. 21 Dec. 1787 and later lived at Cuin (= Peinmollach).

McLean, Finlay (b.1821) bpt. at Aintuim KLN s. of Alexander McLean & Catherine Kennedy.

McLean, Flory (c.1763-1857) wid. 94 d. 23 Sep. 1857 at Oskamull KLN, dau. of Archd. McArthur tenant & Mary Lamont. Bur. Kilvickewen, Ulva. Although her sister Cirsty MacArthur gave info., her age at death is exaggerated, as her parents were m. 1769.

McLean, Flora (c.1775-1870) wid. of **Lachlan McDonald**, dau. of Neil McLean & Marion McLucais, she d. at Fanmore KLN of the infirmities of old age on 26 Feb. 1870 aged 95. Neil McDonald, a friend, gave info and signed with a X.

McLean, Flora (c.1776-1876) m. **Donald McEachern**, lived in Ardtun, Ross of Mull, KLF and d. aged 100, when her f.'s name was given as Allan Maclean, but no mo. could be remembered.

McLean, Flory (c. 1778-1861) wid. of **Lachlan McLean** crofter, dau. of Hugh Rankin miller & Mary Rankin, M/S Rankin, shed. 1 Jun. 1861 at Penmore KLN aged 83 of the infirmities of old age. Mary McLean, dau. present. In **CEN KLN 1861** at Penmore Flory is a wid. 83, crofter b. MRV with dau. Cirsty 36, gr.-dau. Christina 6, gr.-son Lachlan 3, gr.-son John 1. See McLean, Lachlan (c.1774-1860).

McLean, Flora (1784-1885) b. Gribun, dau. of Hugh McLean of Ardchrishnish KLF and Marion McLean, the latter a dau. of Donald McLean of Raodle & Ann, dau. of Donald McLean of Torloisk. She m. **Archibald McLean** s. of John, s. of Lachlan McLean in Kirkipol, Tiree. She d. at Grianal, Tiree in August 1885 aged 101. This was a dau. of Hugh McLean of Ardchrishnish & Marion, dau. of Donald McLean Raodle & Ann McLean dau. of Donald McLean 5th of Torloisk, so she was the dau. of the person whom Allan Torloisk called the "Mull half gentry". **JC/MIP**. p. 359 n.46

Maclaine, Flora (1796-1869) 'Flory Lochbuy' dau. of Murdoch Maclaine 19th of LB & Jane Campbell of Airds. She m. (1) **Allan Maclean** (q.v.) 'the red-haired doctor' (c.1759-1827) when he was 54 and she was 16, and, after his death, and with his express permission to embark on a second marr. (2) **Dr William Whiteside** (1793-1862) of Ayr. There were 9 ch. from her 1st union, John Allan 1814, Murdoch 1815, Donald 1817, Jane 1818, John 1819, Neil (q.v.) 1820, Alexandrina Christina 1822, Christian 1824 & Lachlan Macquarie Maclean 1826. Her 2 daus. from her 2nd marr. were Margaret Dalrymple Whiteside 1832 & Flora C. Whiteside 1834. See Maclean, Neil (1820-1909) her s. A collection of her letters is in **GD174/1634 JC/MIP**.

Maclaine, Flora Anne (c.1799) lived in Edinburgh, Fyfe Place - "*Miss Flora, a handsome girl*" niece of 'Cousin Donald' Maclaine (q.v.) a small-minded nephew of Murdoch Maclaine 19th of LB, and seedsman in Edinburgh. She was Cousin Donald's heir, and m. in the late 1820s a Mr. **McLachlan**, but apparently d. young, or has not been traced. **JC/MIP**.

McLean, Flora (b.1804) dau. of John Maclean of Langamull (drowned 1810) she m. at Kingharair **Peter McArthur** of Ardura 28 Dec. 1824. She was a sister of Ann Maclean who m. John Maclean (q.v.) tacksman of Tiroran. Two different witnesses testified to her misfortune in her choice of a husb. whose drinking was prodigious: "*Peter McArthur has crawled this length tonight. Such a figure may I never see- I cannot tell how I pity his poor wife when she sees him,*" wrote Flory Lochbuy in 1828. Lauchlan Maclaine commented that she had been unlucky in her marr. compared to her sister. Another sister was Margaret Smith McLean (q.v.) who m. Simon Fraser.

McLean, Flora (bpt.1805-1863) she d. of apoplexy 8 Mar. 1863 at 150 Buccleuch Street, Glasgow, wid. of **George Black** mercht., TBR, info from John M. Jones, 34 W. Claremont St., Glasgow. There are testamentary papers for George Black (d.1860) in **NAS**. Her parents were Lachlan McLean (q.v.) farmer & Janet Cameron. Her ch. were Alexander, Joanna, George, Lachlan-Charles, Kenneth & Jessie who m. William Sproat, a procurator fiscal in TBR.

Maclean, Capt. Francis (<1790) "*Capt.Francis Maclaine left this today. He is in very bad health. Sandy Pennycross was with him for some days…*" letter Jane Campbell (Maclaine) of Lochbuy to her s. in Edinburgh, 3 Nov. 1813. **NAS/GD174**. The identity of this Capt. Francis is unknown.

McLean, George (c.1790-1877) m. to **Cirsty McDonald** <1815. See McLean, John, sailor, who d. 1876 at Burg, KLN aged 50. By his 1st marr. George had Malcolm (1815), Flora (1817), Donald (q.v. 1819), Hugh (1821), Coll (1823 – q.v.), Archibald (1826). Bpts. of John c.1828 & Chirsty c.1833 lost in GK. He m., secondly, Sarah McNeill (c.1816-1889), prob. c. 1850-51 by whom he had a dau. Sarah (q.v.). Lived at Burg, Cragaig & Glackugary, all places in same area of KLN. George was s. of Archibald Maclean & Flora Maclean.One of his descendants is the Mull place-names expert Charles Maclean.

McLean, George (bpt.1805) to Neil McLean & Jean Allan in Scallastle TRS. The f. d.1805, for George's bro. Neil McLean was bpt. 27 Feb. 1806 to Jean Allan, 'relict' of Neil McLean.

McLean, George (b.1807) 5th s. of Hector McLean of Ensay & Helen Campbell who had m. in 1800, his mo. being the dau. of Donald Campbell, Chamberlain of Tiree. George was later tenant of Hynish in Tiree. In 1842 he m. Miss **Duncan Malcolm Campbell** [marr. contract in NAS GD1/1003/21 – a very beautiful copperplate document for any descendant to discover!] dau. of Malcolm Campbell & Giles McLachlan. . The couple lived at Ardnacross for a time, and there are some bpts. in **SLN OPR** – of John Archibald in 1848 and George in 1850.

McLean, George (b.1853) s. of Archibald McLean cottar in Kilninian & Mary McInnes. He appears in **CEN 1861 KLN** aged 8, with siblings John 10, Ann 6, Coll 4, Charles 2 & Christina 1. In 1871 he is a farm servt. at Torloisk, enumerated in household of Duncan Munro, under-factor of the estate. In 1881 he is back with his parents in Tostary, and this time his siblings are Ann 26, Christina 20, Catherine 18, Malcolm 16 and Mary 14, all of them unm.– many mouths for his 54-year-old f. to feed.

Maclaine,Gillean (1724-1788) nat. s. of John Maclaine, 17th of Lochbuy he m. **Marie McQuarrie**, dau. of Lachlan McQuarrie of Ulva in 1771 and had 12 ch., Allan (q.v.) 1772, Alicia (q.v.) 1774, Julian (q.v.-girl) 1775, Archibald & Murdoch twins 1777, John 1778, Hector 1780 (d. in infancy), Mary 1782 (d. at 3 days), Flora 1783, Hector 1785, Mary 1787, Margaret Ann (q.v.) 1788. **JPM/HCM** says he was "*esteemed as a benevolent and honorable man*" but recent research in formerly unknown papers at **GRO/Glouc.** show him attempting to alter the legal destination of the estate of LB, removing charter chests by stealth, and deceiving his f. on legal matters. He possibly fabricated the Lochbuy Entail in 1774, causing divisions in the LB family for 100 years. He was however, a competent lawyer, and may have been sorely tried by the fecklessness of many Mull lairds. **JC/MIP**.

McLean, Gillean (1774) may be s. of Flory Rose, a wid. in **ERC/Inhabitants 1779** at Bunessan KLF. But a man of this name from Uisken m. 23 Feb. 1819 **Mary McGilvra** in Siaba and had John (1819), Catherine (1821), Allan (1824) and Janet (1826).

Maclaine, Gillean (1798-1840) coffee planter & exporter, s. of Allan Maclaine (q.v.) of Scallastle & Marjory Gregorson, gr-s. of Gillean Maclaine (1724-1788). Lost at sea returning from Java in the *Regina Victoria* with his Dutch w., 1 son & 2 daus. An able, intelligent, educated, admirable man, he is one of the great might-have-beens of Mull or MRV history, as with his fortune he might have injected capital into both areas, having the idea of buying a Highland estate. **JC/MIP**

McLean, Gillean (b.1803) s. of Abram McLean (q.v.) and Catherine McKie, Tobermory.

McLean, Gillean (c.1827) servt. boy in **CEN KLF 1841** at Saorphein, aged 14. He may be one of the family of Gillean McLean & Mary McGilvra in Siaba, as he works for Duncan McGilvray 60, a gr.f.

McLean, Grace (b.1822) dau. of Charles McLean (q.v.) & Mary McLucash in Penmore. **KLN OPR**

McLean, Grizel (b.1772) bpt. at Aros dau. of Charles McLean (q.v.) & Isabel McGilvray at Gortenbuy (Glencannel). The name Grizel could be rendered as Grace, Giles, Julia, Julian. **KLN OPR**.

McLaine, Hannah (1776-1855) dau. of John McLaine tailor & farmer at Cameron & Catherine McDonald, she m. **Duncan McGilvray**. She d. at Burg in 1855 aged 79. No issue.

McLean, Hannah (c.1848-1919) dau. of Hector McLean tenant farmer & Kate Lamont according to her CRM to **John McFarlane** Iona on 5 Jan. 1876 when she was a wid. 28 called Hannah McKinnon. She d. Iona 1 Nov. 1919 aged 74, her s. Archie McFarlane giving info.

Maclaine, Harriet (b.1798) 'Henrietta', 7th dau. of Murdoch Maclaine (q.v.) 19th of LB and Jane Campbell. She m. 1823 **John Stewart** of Fasnacloich, who had acted "*in the most unhandsome & irregular manner*" to members of her family. 'Fasnacloich' d. 1844.

Maclean, Hector (1703-1784) of Gruline, only s. of Lachlan Maclean of Gruline & Janet Macleod of Bernera, he m. **Catherine**, dau. of Donald **Maclean** of Coll. Their dau. Mary (a.k.a. Christina) was the 'Miss Maclean' admired by Dr Johnson. Served in the army, lived and practised in Glasgow, then worked in Mull, living at Erray nr. TBR. Not known to have any descendants, as Miss Maclean, becoming Mrs McKenzie late in life, was childless.

McLean, Hector (1714-c.1801) tacksman at Ardfenaig, usually known as 'Killean', he appears in **ERC/Inhabitants 1779** at Ardfenaig KLF aged 65, with John 9, Neil 6 and his w. and maids totalling 6 females. According to **AMS/CG** he was the s. of John McLean and Catherine McLean of Kilmory. He served in the army, and m. **Janet McLean** of Shuna late in life. Their ch. were Donald (q.v.) who lived in New Brunswick, Dugald (q.v.) who succeeded as tacksman of Ardfenaig, Neil who d. in 1804 without issue, then John, Catherine, Jessie, Jane (q.v.) Eleanor and Anne. There are many comments about his profligacy in Maclean correspondence, and he was said to be pursued by creditors, but this was not unusual among Mull Macleans.

Maclean, Hector (c.1718-1765) 6th of Torloisk, s. of Donald Maclean (q.v.) of Tarbert & Torloisk & Mary Campbell of Sunderland. His f. d. in 1748 and Hector succeeded as laird of Torloisk but spent most of his time as a 'Writer' or solicitor in Edinburgh., apparently something of a dandy. He was interested in agricultural experiments, cultivation of clovers, flax & corn. Set up a spinning-school for daus. of his tenants, and '*lived genteely among the first company in Scotland*'. After his death, his closet in James's Court, Edinburgh contained 2 suits of claret cloth, 1 white suit, 9 new ruffled shirts and 25 half-worn shirts. Unm., he was succeeded at Torloisk by his bro. Lachlan (q.v.) about whom he had been scoffing in life. He was said to have a nat.dau., perhaps Alicia McLean. **JC/MIP. TP**

McLean, Hector (c.1720-1790s ?) of Torran; s. of Charles of Killunaig & Marion McLean (sister of Donald Torloisk) he m. **Julian McLean**. 2 of their sons, Allan & John (q.v.) were in Jamaica, but dissolved their business partnership; Allan d. Dec. 1783 in America. Alexander ('Sandy Torran') &

Archy were fitted out for Jamaica in 1773. His girls were less adventurous, marrying local men. Mary m. Lachlan Ban Maclean (q.v.) Bunessan; Alicia m. Archibald Maclean of Pennycross; Anne m. Alexander McKinnon Derriguaig.

Maclean, Hector (c.1739) parents not known, he m. **Catherine McDonald** and it is clear from the **CRD** of their s. Donald Maclean at the age of 97 in 1861 in Iona that he must have been m. before 1765. Another s. Archibald (m. to Christina McEachern) d. in 1860 at Ardchiavaig aged 93.

Maclaine, Hector (<1742-1745) 'the infant' 16th of Lochbuy, s. of Lachlan Maclaine & Katharine McDougall. See **JC/MIP**

McLean, Hector (<1745) – prob. KLF; m. to **Christian McArthur** 6 Jan. 1778, and their ch. are recorded in **KLN OPR** although several were b. in KLF <1792- John, Archibald, Mairon and Flora. In 1795 they were in Raodle, KLN, where Lauchlan & John were bpt. But some bpts. not recorded, e.g. Neil McLean (c.1784-1876) who d. at Fanmore in 1876 with these parents.

McLean, Hector (<1760) m. **Flora Brown** <1783, prob. lived at Fidden, KLF. See McLean, Julian (c.1784-1862).

McLean, Hector (<1750) was in Aintuim KLM when he m. **Kathrine McInnes** 4 Sep. 1773, and moved to Kingharair where Florence (1774), Donald (1776), John (1778), Anne (1780) and Charles (1785) were bpt.

Maclaine, Hector (<1760) was in Achacharra at the time of his marr. 6 Feb. 1781 to **Catherine McPherson** in Lephein. At the end of that year their 1st s. Charles was bpt. at Achacharra, then Patrick in 1786, and at Peinmollach, John 1789, Christina 1792, Finlay 1798, Allan 1802, Annabel 1803 & Neil 1806.

McLean, Hector (c.1765) army pensioner at Aird of Penmore in 1789 when his w. **Mary Lamont** had a s. Allan. **CRD** of Anne Menzies, Kilbrenan 1860 aged 74 gives these parents and **CEN KLN 1861** has her b. at Fort George, showing Hector had served there c.1786.

McLean, Hector (<1770) 'Eachann Ruadh' of Ensay & Mingary, KLN. Poss. s. of '*the strong man of Raodle*' Donald McLean (q.v.) & his w. Anne Maclean of Torloisk. On 16 Jun. 1796, Lieut. Hector McLean, Ensay & Ann McDonald had a nat. s. Lauchlan bpt., and 4 yrs. later Hector was m. to Miss **Helen Campbell** dau. of Mr Donald Campbell, Chamberlain of Tiree. From 1800 began the begetting of 11 ch., Donald, Archibald, William, Hector, George, Duncan, Lachlan Allan in 1809 after the move to Mingary,Mary Ann, Anne, Isabella and Janet Catherine. Hector (Eachann Ruadh) is mentioned in *Na Baird Thirisdeach*, or *Tiree Bards* and in Sandy Campbell's report of his travels in Mull in **JC/MIP**. See also McLean, Mary Ann (1811-1894) his dau.

McLean, Hector (<1770) – his name prob. spelt Maclaine – m. **Flory McPhail** and lived in Garmony TRS in the 1790s and 1800s. Some of their ch. were Lachlan (1794), Donald (1799), Anne (1701), Donald (1804), Neil (1807). But little else is known of them.

McLean, Hector (<1770) m. **Janet Campbell** 7 Feb. 1792 when in Baliachtrach KLN. Few baptisms in OPR. Jean in 1792 got them off to a quick start but it is not clear if Isobel bpt. Dervaig in 1807, or Donald McLean (q.v.) b.c. 1794 are of the same stock.

McLean, Hector (1772-1846) s. of Peter McLean of Lag & Christian Lamont, bpt. 12 Jan.1772. He m. **Flora McArthur** (1785-1879) dau. of Donald McArthur tenant in Burg KLN before 1814, and lived at Drumgigha, where the following ch. were bpt: Donald (q.v.) 1814, Malcolm 1816, Margaret 1817, Ann 1819, Mary 1821, Flory 1823, Patrick or Peter (q.v.) 1826. All of these except Malcolm were in **CEN KLN 1841** at Kingharair. By 1851, Flora was a wid. 64 with her s. Donald 35, Mary 26, young Flora 24, Peter 22 and John (q.v.) 19 (whose bpt. c.1829 is lost in GK). Donald bought the island of Gometra in 1857. In 1871 he and his bro. Peter are resident in Gometra House. Flora d. in 1879 aged 93 at Kingharair. Her s. Donald d. 8 Aug.1871. John d. at Gometra 17 Jan. 1893 aged 63, and Peter d. at Kingharair 4 May 1893 aged 67. **GRV Calgary**. These sons were all unm., and it was left to the daus. to carry on the line. Margaret McLean m. Neil Rankin Morrison (1811-1900), Aintuim, later in Cuin and Tobermory(of the Rankin piping family – his mo. being Neil Rankin's dau.) and was mo. of at least 8 ch., incl. Cowan or Conduillie Rankin Morrison (1856 – 1943) the antiquarian.
SWHIHR Notes & Queries vi March 1978. OPR Kiln. GRV Calgary.

McLean, Hector (<1775) m. **Anne McLean** and lived in Fishnish TRS where Mary, Marion, John & Flory were bpt. in the early 1800s. In c.1828-9 when LMD compiled his *List of Souls* he noted a

Hector Maclaine 55 in Fishnish with Mrs Maclaine 52, Flory 24, Jessy 19 & Chirsty 15 – near enough to this Hector's family in age. 12 yrs later **CEN TRS 1841** has a handloom weaver, Hector McLean 60 and his w. Ann 60 looking like our couple and with one dependant Flora aged 9, probably gr.-ch. In 1851 Hector is 80 and a pauper living with dau. Christian &gr.-dau. Peggy Currie.

McLean, Hector (<1775) belonged to Kilmore, part of KLN centred on Dervaig, and m. an **Isabel McLean** <1804. Their ch. from 1804 were Allan 1804, Lachlan 1807, Flory 1809, Donald 1812, Hector 1814, John 1819, Margaret 1822, & Elizabeth. But with Elizabeth's bpt. 1824 we go into the darkness of the Kilninian Gap (see preface) and have to rely on **CEN KLN 1841** of Dervaig to reconstruct part of family. In Bellachroy Hector is 60, 'Bell' 55 and John 20. In **CEN KLN 1851**, Kilbeg, nr. Bellachroy, Hector is gone, Bell is a wid. 68 b. Torasa (ie the farm of that name, not TRS), John her s. is 30, m. to Anne 30 b. Coll, and there are 2 gr-ch. John 2 & Flory 1. Isabella McLean d. 25 Jan. 1858 at Kilbeg aged 77. She was dau. of John McLean tenant in Torasa & Anne McLean M/S McLean. Perhaps just a little too much Maclean blood here!

McLean, Hector Hugh (c.1780-1840) s. of Lachlan Ban McLean (q.v.) of Bunessan & Mary McLean of Torrans, he served in the 93rd Regt. of Foot, being severely wounded c.1815. He had a nat. s. Hugh by Catherine McGilvra, servt. girl in Bunessan bpt. 20 Mar. 1818 and m. **Ann McLeod** (b.1778) dau. of the Rev. Neil McLeod 30 Apr. 1818, (with that insensitive haste shown by so many Mull men who thus tried their virility before marr.) when she was 40. She bore him 3 ch., Margaret Burnett (m. George Grierson, Aberfeldy), Lachlan Allan (went to America in 1842 and was stabbed to death in 1864) and Mary Sibella b. 1821 at Carsaig m. the Rev. Duncan Blair, Pictou, NS. Hector Hugh was involved in an acrimonious dispute with Murdoch Maclaine of LB over the condition of the house he rented at Carsaig. Being as litigious as most of his tribe, and also being involved in a strangely virulent legal action brought by the Rev. Mr Alexander Fraser, he was bankrupted by the costs. Donald Maclean WS (q.v.) began by approving of 'Capt. McLean', but before long was regretting his trust, and posting a horning for the recovery of £175 from Hector: *"this must be ruin to the ABSURD MAN... he thinks he can save the money by its being in his wife's name but he will find himself egregiously*

mistaken…" Run to ground by the combined forces of the Mull establishment, Donald WS, Murdoch Lochbuy, Col. Campbell of Knock & the Macleans of Coll, Capt. Hector spent the remainder of his days in Kintyre. After his death, his wid. Ann McLeod rejoined her sisters Mary & Susan (q.v.) at Springbank TBR. Maclean historians like **AMS & JPM** like to pretend he went to Kintyre for the sake of his ch.'s education, but they believed the best of their kinsmen, and did not have access to the LB Papers. Capt. Hector's letters are aggressive, churlish and over-bearing, but he may have been injured in every sense, and in a later age would have been able to sue the Army Office for Post Traumatic Stress Disorder.　　　　　**NAS**　　　**GD174/1653/1-9 GD174/1628/329-36**

McLean, Hector (c.1789-1869) unm. sailor who d. aged 80 in Tobermory in 1869, s. of Alexander McLean feuar & Christina Fletcher.

McLean, Hector (1794-1868) s. of Neil McLean & Catherine McInnes (see entry for his bro. Andrew, tailor) he remained a bachelor and lived latterly at Ardalanish, near his bro. John McLean.

McLean, Hector (c.1804-1883) crofter in Dervaig, m. to **Margaret McLean** (q.v.- c.1809-1892). In **CEN KLN 1861** at 13 High Street,Dervaig Village, they were Hector McLane [sic] 57, feuar, b. Ardnacross, with Margaret 51 b. Bellachroy. Alexander,25b. Penmollach; John22b. Ardow; Ann 14 & Margaret 12 both 'scholars' b. Dervaig. He was s. of Archibald McLean and Ann McDougall.

McLean, Hector (b.c.1805) from Achadashenaig SLN when he m. 24 Jun. 1835 **Catherine Fletcher**, dau. of the overseer of Fidden KLF & Catherine McLean (q.v.). Their 1st ch. were twins Robert & Mary bpt. 25 June 1836. In Dec. 1838 when they were at Ariglass, Alexander was bpt. Catherine in 1840, Flora in 1843, Hugh c.1845, Duncan c. 1847, Ann c.1849, Archibald c. 1850.

McLean, Hector (<1808) in **CEN KLN 1871** and **1881** a Hector McLean is a crofter in Dervaig with a w. named **Margaret** and several dependants. His dau. Margaret has had the misfortune to be widowed before the age of 22, and she is Margaret McDougall in **CEN KLN 1871**, already with a 3-year-old dau. Mary and 7-mo.-old James. Hector's s. Alexander, b.c. 1843, is a gardener, still unm. at the age of 38 in 1881.

McLean, Hector (c.1810-c.1843) s. of Neil

McLean (q.v.) & [Flora McLean ?] he was in **CEN KLN 1841** Kilmore when his f. was 60 and Hector 30. Hector's w. was **Janet McInnes**, who was a wid. in **CEN KLN 1851**, aged 35. We know he had a s. Donald (c.1842-1859) who d. at Aintuim aged 17, but GK makes it difficult to trace other ch.

McLean, Hector (1811-1869) s. of Donald McLean tenant in Iona and Flora McFee, bpt. 19 May 1811 and m. **Grace or Grizzel Lamont** 24 Mar. 1846. Their ch. were retrospectively registered in 1855 in **ION QS OPR**, but **CEN KLF 1861** gives a better picture of the family at Sligeanach, Iona, headed by the patriarchal Donald McLean (q.v.) aged 96 and his w. Flora McFee 86. Hector their s. was 46 with Grace 30, and their ch. were Lachlan 13, Catherine 11, Chirsty 9, Donald 6, Mary 5, Margaret 1. There were 2 more ch. Flora and Dugald (1865). The gr.f. was to die only 1 month or 2 after the census of 1861 aged 97, and Hector did not match his longevity, dying at Iona 26 May 1869 aged 58 of asthma. He was succeeded in Sligeanach by his s. Lachlan, and then by his gr.-s. Hector, who d. unm. in 1956. Grace Lamont was the dau. of Donald Lamont crofter & Catherine McArthur. She d. at the Argyll Hotel, Iona in 1907 at the age of 86.

McLean, Hector (1813-1896) bpt. 31Jan.1813, s. of John McLean & Flory McLeod in Dervaig KLM. He m. **Catherine McDonald** (c.1818-1886). His mo. Flora was only ch. in OPR of Donald McLeod and Margaret Rankin (1768-1855 - dau. of Hector Rankin and Elizabeth McLachlan). Hector was a grocer in Dervaig, and in **CEN KLN 1851** he is said to be 36, his wid. gr.-mo. Margaret McLeod, nee Rankin living in his house aged 83. Hector's s. John also became a mercht. at Dervaig (see family GRVs at KLM for Catherine McDonald who d. 4 Jul. 1886 & others). A s., Peter McLean MD. JP. d. at Glenview, Dervaig in 1940, and had been the physician present at Hector's death in 1896.

McLean, Hector (c.1843-1915) s. of John McLean (q.v.) shepherd & Anne McArthur, b. Torasa-Quinish, but without a bpt. record, he was 8 in **CEN KLN 1851** at Torasa-Quinish, and 18 in **CEN KLN 1861**. He was a shepherd in Lettermore when he m. **Betsy Clark** in Jun. 1868. She was 25, b. Torness TRS dau. of John Clark shepherd & Janet McPherson (both b. mainland Argyll). Hector & Betsy began their marr. lives at

Crannich inland from Aros Bridge where their 1st s. John was b.1870, then moved to Balevulen KLF where Mary Ann, Lachlan, Duncan, Neil and another were b. A description exists of both Hector & Betsy McLean from Iona Houston's *Memories of Mull*. She was Iona McVean, and the McVean family were tenants of Killiemore House. Iona McVean wrote, after 1912, "*Our shepherd, Hector McLean, was a great character. He spoke very little English. He must have been a very fit and strong man, for he scoured the hills from morning to night with his three very clever dogs, rounding up sheep and watching over them. He trained two of them in Gaelic and one in English, a very clever idea. He had the most wild war whoop he used to let off at the dogs when they were getting out of range. It carried for miles and always thrilled us as children – it had such a blood-curdling sound about it. He hated killing sheep for us, and complained bitterly when we had many visitors and required more than one sheep a week, and was once heard to say 'If I were to kill the Devil himself and hang him up in the safe, they would eat him at Kilfinichen!' We had 1,400 sheep at Kilfinichen, and Hector said he knew each individually..."* Iona McVean also described Betsy McLean: *"She must have been lovely as a girl, and was still lovely as an elderly woman, wearing a spotless swatch on her head, a little tartan shawl crosswise over her shoulders, a short 'drugget' skirt. She was a most capable and clever woman and very clever intellectually. She could show up anyone in a second and was always right too! We always loved a visit to her, sitting by her cosy kitchen fire listening to her stories of long ago...She had a very good-looking family of four boys and two girls... she thumped cloth... sang waulking songs...a great spinner... looked so charming at her spinning wheel!"* Hector d. as a retired shepherd at Rohill, Glenforsa 28 Apr. 1915 aged 72. His s. Lachlan, a shopkeeper in Salen, unm. aged 40, gave info on his f., and less than 6 mo. later was found in Glenforsa having d. of exposure on 11 Dec. 1915.

McLean, Hector (c.1845-1861) d. aged 16 at Dervaig KLN 1861. His f. was Lachlan McLean, crofter, his mo. Marion Macdonald. In **CEN KLN 1861** at Dervaig Lachlan McLean is a feuar 52, b. Kilbeg with Marion w. 54 b. Anabost, Donald 18 b. Dervaig & this Hector 15 b. Dervaig.

McLaine, Helen (c.1795) m. **John McLaine** (q.v.) in Fishnish TRS in 1815. See McLean, Ann, her dau., bpt. 1815.

McLean, Hugh (<1745) in Sorne KLN <1768 m. to **Christian McPherson**, their 1st ch. in **KLN OPR** was unnamed in 1768, then they had Mary 1770, Alexander 1772,John 1775, Hugh 1777, Florence 1780, Duncan 1782, Ann 1785. Duncan d. TBR 1856 aged 77 of consumption.

McLean, Hugh (<1760) miller & crofter, Penmore m. **Mary Campbell**. See CRD of their dau. Peggy McLean (c.1785-1860)

Maclaine, Hugh (c.1760?) vintner in Tobermory, bro. of Dr. Andrew & Dr. Donald Maclaine; unable to take charge of his dec. bro.'s concerns in 1797; employed a tutor (Donald McNeill) for his ch., Peter, John, Isabella, Marguerite, Donald, Hugh & Andrew. Isabella (q.v.) m. Robert Cuthbertson. He took farm of Kingharair from Mrs Clephane Whitsunday 1813, and Kilmanie [?] which "*causes him to be very much from home looking out for stocking to these lands – tenements to build also – which is no easy job at present, wood & other material being so high. We intend to leave this house at Whitsunday first*." [Isabella Maclaine to Peter Maclaine, 65th Regt. of Foot, Bombay, 6 Sept. 1813, from Tobermory]. Hugh may be the HM in New Inn of Tobermory m. to **Flora McLachlan**. If so their ch. were bpt. Mary 1794, Andrew 1796, Donald 1798.

McLean, Hugh (<1765) miller in Penmore KLN, he m. (1) **Mary McDonald** in 1781 and (2) **Flora Morrison**. He bred several millers from both wives, indeed was responsible for a dynasty of millers, his 1st s. John McLean (q.v.) succeeding his f. in Penmore.

Maclaine, Hugh (1781-1828) s. of Farquahar Maclaine (q.v.) and Betty Macquarie (sister of Lachlan Macquarie, governor of NSW) he was bpt. 20 Jul. 1781. Assumed name of Murdoch Hugh, Ensign 73rd Regt. 29 Nov. 1795 [as Murdoch] Lieut. 77th Regt. [as Murdoch Hugh] 5 May 1799, Capt. 3 Jul. 1805, Major 20 May 1813 brevet Lieut.-Col. 15 Aug. 1822, Lieut.-Col. 26 Dec. 1822 having served in Walcheren 1809 & in the Peninsula 1811-14 [right leg amputated Ciudad Rodrigo, pension from 20 Jun.1813] on elder bro.'s death went to Jamaica with 42nd, d. unm. 1828. A nat. dau. Mary was bpt. 1826 to "*Lieut.-Col. H. McLaine, 77th Regt. and Peggy McQuarie in Oskamull*". **KLN OPR; GRO LMD**

McLean, Hugh (c.1782-1860) s. of Charles McLean farmer & Marion Currie, he was a weaver, pauper, wid., d. 13 Apr. 1860 Tobermory aged 78.

McLean, Hugh (bpt. 1802) s. of Allan McLean (q.v.) & Flora McDougall in Braes of Lagganulva (Torloisk Estate). Emig. to Australia (to join relations) with w. Sarah & ch. soon after 1851 census where their ages were Hugh 48, **Sarah** ('Merron') 38, John 17, Catherine 15, Donald 12, Archibald 7, Allan 4. Marr. (prob. c.1833) and bpts. lost in GK.

Maclean, Hugh (1808-1863) 2nd s. to be named Hugh of Alexander McLean (q.v.) farmer & Flora McGilvray. A mercht. in Iona, he m. 14 Jun. 1836 **Effy Maclean**, dau. of Lachlan McLean farmer & Catherine McLean. In **CEN ION 1851** he was a grocer, E. End, Iona aged 40 with Euphemia 38 (b. Acharn KLN 1810), Margaret 12, Lachlan 10, Mary 4 mo. Hugh d. at Martyr's Bay on 4 Nov. 1863 aged 55 of heart disease.His wid. Effy 58 was in **CEN KLF 1871** in 'SHOP' Iona Village with her s. Lachlan & dau. Margaret at Iona Cottage next door. Effy d. 2 Jan. 1875 at the age given by a farm servt. as 59, but in fact was nearer 64. Lachlan their s. (q.v.) (1839) continued the family business.

McLean, Hugh (bpt.1818) nat. s. of Capt. Hector Hugh McLean & Catherine McGilvray bpt. 20 Mar. 1818, one mo. < his f. m. Miss Ann McLeod. **KLF OPR**

McLean, Hugh (1826) twin s. (with Neil bpt. at Penmore) of John McLean & Catherine McKinnon of the great family of millers & blacksmiths in Penmore & Dervaig. The adult Hugh is first encountered in **CEN KLN 1851** at Dervaig, blacksmith aged 24 with a new young w. Marion 18, & his younger bro. Lachlan 18 as his apprentice. But a CRB in which Marion/Sarah's f. Malcolm Beaton (b. Killundine MRV 1800 m. 1823 Janet McDonald Aintuim) as gr.f. gives info. in 1862 has their date of marr. as Feb. 1852. The marr. with **Sarah Beaton** was prob. Feb. 1851, lost in GK. She had been bpt. at Aintuim KLN 22 Jan. 1826. In **CEN KLN 1881** at Dervaig Hugh is 52, his w. Marion 46, Alexander 25, Mary Ann 23, Donald 21, Jessie 19, John 17, Malcolm 13, Charles 11, Betsy 8 & Sarah 1. Another dau. Flora b.c.1852 stayed with gr.parents in 1861 census.

McLean, Hugh (1843-1917) another of the Penmore millers, gr.s. of Hugh McLean (<1765) & his 2nd wife Flora Morrison, s. of Donald McLean & Mary McLean in Penmore & Kellan.

Maclaine, Ishbel (c.1765- after 1804) nat. dau. of Murdoch Maclaine 19th of Lochbuy, she was brought up in Edinburgh, the name of her mo.

being unknown, and indeed her existence was announced to the trustees after the death of her f. in 1804, when, because Murdoch had never mentioned her, support was refused. She m. 15 Feb. 1788 **James Neilson**, an Edinburgh coppersmith, and their 1st s., Murdoch, was bpt. 13 Aug. 1788. There was also a dau. Jean in 1791 and a son James in 1795. None of these descendants has so far been traced. **JC/MIP**

McLean, Isabel (c.1780?-1832) dau. of Charles McLean of Scour & Catherine McLean of Muck she m. the Rev. **Edmund McQueen** as his 2nd w. 20 May 1801 and had a s. named Charles b. 1803. She d. 26 Nov.1832. McQueen is described in Hall's Travels and d. 1812. **FES AMS/CG**

Maclaine, Isabella (<1795) dau. of Hugh Maclaine (q.v.) or McLean, vintner, Tobermory and later farmer at Kingharair. She m. **Robert Cuthbertson** fishery officer TBR 2 Oct. 1814. Daus Flora 1815 and Barbara 1817. In James Johnson's THE RECESS or AUTUMNAL RELAXATION IN THE HIGHLANDS 1834, he says "*our rejectment into the streets threw us into the comfortable house of Mrs Cuthbertson (in Tobermory), seated on an eminence, and commanding a most romantic prospect.*" Isabella had sasine 1823 of a dwelling house on the north side of the street in Portmore. **JC/MIP**

Maclean, Isabella (c.1846-1886) this was her marr. name, middle name Alexandrina, m. to **Archibald John Maclean** (q.v.) of PX. She d. aged 40 on 8 Feb. 1886, at Carsaig KLF. Her f.was Henry Simon, her mo. Juliet Rodyk. Early death due to congestion of brain resulting from exhaustion following a confinement (b. of Violet in 1885).She had been m. previously, and info on her death was given by her dau. Isabelle Griswold.

McLean, James (<1720) nat. s. of Donald McLean (1671-1725) of Brolass, he m. **Julia McLean** or Maclaine, dau. of Allan Maclaine of Garmony and sister of John Lochbuy. He had at least 3 surviving ch. before being killed in America c.1758- John, Hugh, Julian (q.v.). His s. John had 5 ch., and John's s. Allan who was in coal mining in Ayrshire is supposed to have had 1 s., Allan Og, and 9 daus. Allan Og is said to have gone to Pictou & Pennsylvania and to have had 4 sons, Allan, Andrew, Alexander & James. Julia & James's line, stemming from a nat. s. flourished like the green bay tree, whilst their cousins found it difficult to supply heirs to Duart & Lochbuy.

McLean, James (c.1770-1850s) *See* McLean,

Margaret (c.1809-1892) his dau. James McLean and **Ann McPhaiden** at Mingary were m. 27 Feb. 1798. Their ch. were bpt. Alexander 22 Dec. 1798; Alexander 12 Oct. 1800; Flora 4 Jan. 1804; Margaret 16 Apr. 1806; John 30 May 1808; Neil 18 Sep.1810; Donald 11 Jul. 1813; Mary 5 Oct. 1815; Janet 15 Feb. 1818. The 1st 2 bpts. were at Mingary, the next 3 at Kilbeg KLN, the following 3 at Achnadrish, the last at Kilbeg. In **CEN KLN 1851** James 84 and Anne 74 are in Drimnacroish, with Neil 30, Donald 28, Jennet 25, all unm., and ages <u>very</u> far out! No sign of family in 1861, but an Alexander d. 1881 at Bellochroy aged 82 with these parents.

McLaine, James (1802-1870s) weaver, poss. s. of John& Effy McLaine in Garmony, he was in Ballyraoich TRS when he m. **Mary McLaine**, Parish of Mearns in June 1837. In 1841 at Garmony they had a dau. Mary 2. In **CEN TRS 1851** James is 48, with Mary 45 and a garland of girls – Mary 12, Euphemia 9, Ann 5, Flora 2. Still in the area in 1871, James is 68, Mary 64, Flora 23, Ann 22, Charles landers gr.-s. 4 and Mary McKellar gr.-dau. 3. All b. TRS so that Mary's stay in the Mearns was prob. for work. James had d. by 1881 when his wid. was a pauper living with her gr.-dau. Mary McKellar.

McLean, James (<1810) youngest s. of Donald McLean (q.v.) and Giles McArthur; servant man to LMD.

McLean, James (b.c.1820) in **CEN TBR 1851** mercht. Tobermory, already a wid. at 30, but with no ch. in his household. His mo. Catherine (b.c.1783) is his housekeeper, both b. Kilchattan.

McLean, Jane (1782-1864) dau. of Lieut. Hector McLean of the Highland Fencibles & Janet McLean of Shuna, she was also younger sister of Capt. Dugald McLean (q.v.) of Ardfenaig (c.1762-1818). She was prob. b. at Ardfenaig where her f. was tacksman in **ERC/Inhabitants 1779** and where her bros. John & Neil were 12 and 9 at the time of her birth. She and her sisters Catherine and Jessie remained unm. Their younger sisters Eleanor & Anne have not been traced. After the accidental drowning of their bro. Dugald in 1818, nothing is known of the sisters' lives apart from a social visit paid by Jane to 'old' Mrs Maclaine of Lochbuy at Scallastle until Jessie & Jane set up house together at Bunessan and appear in **CEN KLF 1851** as joint proprietors of Gowanbrae at Bunessan, when Jessie is 72 and Jane 70. In **CEN KLF 1861** they have grown no older, described as 'government annuitants'. Jane d. at Iona 29 Jan. 1864 aged 82 of influenza, in the house of her niece Susan's husb., the Rev. Donald McVean. These two great aunts were remembered by descendants of the Ardfenaig McLeans, and a photograph exists of Jessie.

Maclaine, Jane (b.1787) 1st ch. of the marr. of Murdoch Maclaine 19th of LB & Jane Campbell of Airds, she disappointed her family by not being the male heir. Her parents were to have 9 daus. and 2 sons. She was looked after by her gr.-mo. for the first few years. Madly in love with the 'unsuitable' James Gregorson, she gave him up in 1815, when Donald Maclean WS (q.v.) had written, "*I have long forgiven Jane in my heart for her unkindness to me... her engagement to James Gregorson is most unfortunate. I wish to God it could honourably be broke off. I spoke to him and he told me everything was settled, but he is involved very much without any hope of being extricated...plunging both in ruin...wish you could speak to her... I will show James the folly of it... every day adds to his ruin here... I do not know how he supports himself...*" The same writer was relieved when Jane m. **Colin Campbell** of Kintraw in 1817. After living at Kintraw they moved to Torrans KLF and later to Duart Cottage, by Duart Castle. Some flaw in Colin's character made him unpopular with both Murdoch Maclaine 20th of LB, his bro.-in-law, and with Col. Campbell of Possil, who had appointed Colin factor. Dismissed in 1831, the couple were in dire straits before arranging to go to Australia in 1839 with ch. Alexander, Mary, Wilmina, Murdoch, John (b.1826) and Donald (b.1829), paying for their passage with a roup of all their possessions. They settled in Adelaide. Their dau. Jean/Jane m. the blind Charles Maclean (q.v.) (1806-1872) s. of Donald Maclean WS in 1837, and lived in Canada. **JC/MIP**

Maclaine, Jane Jarvis (1802-1882) wid. of **Andrew Scott** of Ettrickbank, landed proprietor, she d. 9 Apr. 1882 of heart disease (and sudden apoplexy) at 40 Palmerston Place Edinburgh aged 80, youngest dau. of Murdoch Maclaine of LB, landed proprietor, & Jane Campbell.Info on her death supplied by her niece, BM Gregorson, 4 Greenhill Terrace, Edinburgh. Jane Jarvis in her youth was a colourful character who rode horses and generally behaved in an unladylike manner. She m. Andrew Scott late in life, having had a close attachment to Charles Maclean s. of Donald WS. Her husb. financed several Mull property

deals. **JC/MIP**

McLean, Jane (c.1814-1864) dau. of Charles McLean crofter & Christina Cameron and wid. of **Donald McLean** (q.v.) shoemaker, she d. 22 Mar. 1874 at Oskamull aged 60 of swelling of the feet. Her nephew Lachlan McLachlan was present. Jane McLean and her husb. were b. TRS, their 1st ch. Margaret being bpt. 6 Apr. 1830 at Corrachy, **SLN QS OPR**. For other ch. see Donald her husb.

Maclaine, Jane (1820-1899) single, she d. at Java Lodge TRS, in 1899, aged 79, of paraplegia. Info from her sister Mary Anne Maclaine. The unm. dau. of Murdoch Maclaine 20th of Lochbuy & Chirsty Maclean, dau. of Donald Maclean WS.

McLean, Janet (18th C.) dau. of Hector McLean, Glenbyre & Flora McLean, gr.-dau. of Neil McLean in Fishnish, as wid. of **Hugh McLean** workman in LB, she was beneficiary of Will of Miss Mary McLean (q.v. d.1834) matron of the Town's Hospital, Glasgow.

McLean, Janet (Jessie) (c.1784) of Ardfenaig family. See McLean, Jane (1782-1864) her sister.

McLean, Janet (1789-1869) d. 14 May 1869 at Bunessan aged 80, wid. of **James Morrison**, mercht. Bunessan who had been drowned 2 May 1828. JC/MIP. Sometimes called McLaine, she was of Uisken family, related to Maclaines of LB, dau. of Duncan Maclean and Mary Maclean. Her ch. were Elizabeth bpt. 1816, Catherine 1817, Archibald 1819, Margaret 1821, John 1823, Mary 1825, Alexander 1826, Jemima 1828, b. > her father's death, and named Jemima for him, as was the custom with posthumous ch. Janet was the dau. of Duncan Maclean, farmer & Mary McLean (M/S McLean); she was involved in the legal battle in the case of the Will of Colonel Alexander Maclean of Uisken, her uncle. Her dau. Jemima m. Peter McNaughton rather late in life.

McLean, Janet (1804-1873) another of the Penmore miller family, she m. 1836 **Malcolm McLucais or McDougall**, shoemaker (c.1787-1868). She was 1st dau. of Hugh McLean (<1765)by his 2nd w. Flora Morrison.Her ch., who completed the name-shift to McDougall, were Flora c.1837, Neil c.1839, Hugh c.1842 and Donald c.1846.

McLean, Janet (1820-1905) wid. of **Patrick or Peter McCormick** (1806-1892) she d. Kilmore 1905 aged 84. She was the youngest dau. of Donald McLean (q.v.) and Mary Morrison who had lived at Kilbrenan.

McLean, Jean (c.1815-1878) w. of **Allan Lamont** (c.1810-1897). Nothing in Scottish records suggests anything untoward about a Lamont-McLean marr. which took place at Lagganulva KLN on 29 Feb. 1836 (save that the couple would have few anniversaries) on the same day as bpt. of their ch. Betty. Other ch. Janet 1838, Marianne 1841, Isabella 1843, Murdoch 1845, Angus 1847 and John 1850. But they lived at Oskamull, home of the late Governor Lachlan Macquarie of NSW and his family, and devotees of that family will recognise Macquarie names – Betty for the sister, Marianne for the sister-in-law, Murdoch for the uncle of the famous man. Allan & Jean and their ch. emig. to Australia in 1853 on the *New Zealander* sailing to Portland Bay, and it is in Australian records that we find Jean to be a nat. dau. of Major Murdoch McLean (Maclaine) (q.v.), nephew of the Governor of NSW & Hannah Roebuck. The Roebucks, a remarkable family of English scientists working in Scotland, had enough genius to pass exceptional genes to future generations. The Lamonts were clever enough. Allan Lamont's mo. happened to be a Maclean (Mary McLean m. John Lamont) as was Jean's f. Allan d. at Penhurst, Victoria in 1897, and Jean in 1878. In Australia, descendants of Betsy or Betty Lamont have emerged from her marr. to Frank Liles Olle in 1859, and progeny of the other ch. have still to be discovered.

McLean, Jessie (c.1801-1883) unm. dressmaker dau. of Charles McLean & Isabella Campbell she d. of old age on 19 May 1883 at Portmore, Tobermory aged 82. Informant at her death was Dugald Campbell JP for Argyllshire, her nephew.

Maclaine, John (c.1700-1778) of Lochbuy, s. of Allan Maclaine of Garmony (3rd s. of Hector 12th of Lochbuy) & Julia McLean of Torloisk, he succeeded his f. in Garmony, but had no expectation of the LB title until Hector 16th 'the infant' d. 1745. As the infant's gr.f. John 14th of LB was still alive, having retired to make way for his s. Lachlan 'the Prodigal', John, although next in line, could not succeed until it was certain that 'the Grandfather' would have no more sons, for in 1745 the gr.f. was only about 65. But Isabel McDougall 'the Grandmother' was also in her sixties, so no new heir was engendered. John of Garmony now became the heir presumptive to LB, but when the gr.f. d. in 1748, it became apparent that the estate was riddled with debt, and trustees were appointed to regulate the tiny income allowed to the new Lochbuy. 'John Lochbuy' had

a nat. s., Gillean (q.v.) before he m. in 1842 **Isabel McLean** of Brolass, sister of the man soon to become the new Chief of clan Maclean, Sir Allan McLean. The daus. of John LB & Isobel are of uncertain date, and even uncertain legitimacy, although Isabel & Catherine seem to be Lady Lochbuy's own girls, but their only surviving lawful s. was Archy, b.c.1749. This s. was well educated to become laird of an estate heavy with debt. John LB was litigious and lost many legal cases. He & his wife lived in a small and mean house near the old castle of Moy. They were observed to have only 1 pot. When his adored son Archy went to America, John went into a decline, dying in 1778.He was fortunate not to know of his s.'s murder in 1784. LB was to have no resident laird until Murdoch Maclaine arrived with his bride in 1786. Isabel, old Lady Lochbuy would d. at the end of the 18th C. **JC/MIP**

McLean, John (<1720) from Hysker in N. Uist, he came to live in Mull when he m. **Catherine McLean**, dau. of Rev. John McLean (1680-1756), Maighstir Seathan, min. of Kilninian, and sister of Rev. Alexander McLean, also min. of Kilninian. They lived at Mingary on Quinish estate. Catherine d. 1772, and John returned to Uist 1775. Their s. was the Hon. Neil McLean (1759-1832) who, in a letter of 1814 from Riviere aux Raisins, Canada to his s. Alexander McLean, gives family info.

McLaine, John (1728-1792) of Gruline, s. of Allan Maclaine of Suie & Marion Campbell, tacksman to the LB family, incl. John LB, Archy LB, Gillean Maclaine & Murdoch Maclaine. "*A worthy honest man, much attached to the interest of the family of Lochbuy.*" Lived at Bradil, then Gruline, unm., his sister 'Miss Ketty' keeping house for him. Not to be confused with his nephew John McLean (q.v.) of Gruline, who has that name in **AMS/CG**. AMS did not appear to know of this John. As tacksman, he played a role which was dying out, of go-between for the people and the lairds. He was exploited by Archy, his favourite LB laird.For his nat. s. by Mary McLean see McLean, Archibald (<1740). His letters are in **NAS GD174/1328**.

Maclean, John (c.1729) "Iain Ban Mac Ailein" tenant in Acharn in **ERC/Inhabitants 1779** aged 50; m. **Effy Stewart**, prob. f. of Charles McLean (q.v.), Allan McLean (q.v.) and gr.-f. of Rev. Neil McLean (q.v.) of Ulva. Said to have been in 1745 Jacobite uprising.

Maclean, John (<1740) of Inverscadale, 'Castle Dowart' s. of John Maclean in Sorne & Mary Maclean. He went to Jamaica in 1760 to claim an estate there called Castle Dowart left to him by a cousin, and remained for over 10 yrs, returning to Mull in the 1770s. In 1779 he m. **Sibella**, dau. of Sir Allan **Maclean**. It is difficult to tell whether the epithet 'John Jamaica' is used for him or for John Maclean nephew of John Gruline, but when the title 'Castle Duart' is used by the Maclean correspondents it is not flattering. Of Sir Allan's sons-in-law and their expectations from his legal process, Donald Maclaine wrote "...*Drimnin grips at all this money and Castle Dowart may get a little feel...*" His son d. unm. in W. Indies. His dau. Mary Ann m. Dr Mackenzie Grieve.

McLean, John (c.1745-1810) of Langamull. "Iain Mac Eoghain" m. **Mary McLean**. He was s. of Hugh McLean of Langamull. John Maclean had 9 ch. according to **AMS/CG**: Donald who m. Catherine McLean of Pennycross with no issue; Hugh; Alexander [d. 1821 in East Indies, see above] Lachlan d. young; Mary m. Allan McLean of Crossapol; Ann m. John McLean tacksman of Tiroran; Christy m.Alexander McLean of Kingharair; Flora (q.v.) m. Peter McArthur; Margaret (q.v.) m. Lieut. Fraser. John McLean of Langamull was drowned Feb. 1810. His wife d. Dec. 1811. Margaret was Margaret Smith McLean, who m. Lieut. Simon Fraser of the 4th W. India Regt. of Foot on 1 Dec. 1817 .

MacLaine, John (<1750) tailor & farmer m. **Catherine McDonald**, living in Cameron TRS on LB estate in 1770s.Known from **CRD 1855** of his dau. Hannah MacLaine who d. aged 79, 3 Dec. 1855 at Burg as wid. of Duncan McGilvray, John was also in 1841 census at Cameron aged 90, tailor, with Hannah 55 (who seems to have been childless).

McLean, John (<1750->1800) 'John Gruline' the nephew [when he succeeded his uncle of the same name] he was s. of Hector McLean (q.v.) of Torran & Julian McLean who was sister of John Gruline henchman of Archy, Murdoch & Gillean Maclaine. It is difficult to tell whether he is the unpopular person referred to as 'John Jamaica' or whether this is also a name for John McLean 'Castle Dowart' (q.v.). One is inclined to believe 'John Jamaica' refers to this nephew, as Charles Macquarie wrote: "*My opinion of John Maclaine the more I get acquainted with him the less I think of his integrity.*" He seems to have lived at Torran

until 1795, then at Gruline until this part of LB was sold, settling the accounts of his uncle John Gruline after the latter's death in 1792. He was left a small legacy by his aunt 'Miss Ketty' in 1803, and that is the last we hear of him. There is no mention of a marr., a wife or ch. His letters are in **NAS GD174/1479**

McLean, John (1755-1821) nat. s. of Archibald of Laggan and his 'concubine' Marion McLean, he m. **Flora McQuarrie** dau. of Lachlan McQuarrie of Ulva, and had 4 sons, but no gr.ch. He was known as 'John McLean Kilbrenan' or 'John Laggan'. **JC/MIP**

Maclaine, John (b.1757) also Maclean, tacksman of Tiroran KLF. He is possibly the John who appears in the 1779 census at Torranbeg KLF aged 22 with his bro. Charles 14, in which case he changed his allegiance from the duke of Argyll's estate to Lochbuy's.He m. **Ann**, dau. of John **Maclean** of Langamull, and they had at least 16 ch., all of whom were brought up as 'Ladies and Gentlemen'. There is also reason to think his mo. & 3 sisters were still living with him c.1815, when he left the country. He had arguments with Murdoch Maclaine of LB and Gillean, and was a friend to the oppressed. With 16 ch. to educate, he finally emig. to America with £500, prob. in a company of over 20 of his close family, yet no clues exist as to his destination, fate or descendants. **JC/MIP**

McLean, John (<1755) m. 3 Apr. 1781 when he was in Baliachtrach, **Isobel McKinnon** n.p. Bpts. – Anne 1782 in Sorne; Christian 1788 in Sorne; Donald 1794 in Calve.

McLean, John (<1765) m. 21 Dec. 1787 when he was in Penmollach, **Jean McDonald**. Bpts. in Penmollach or Cuin KLN were: Donald 1788; Neil 1790; Finlay 1791; Catherine 1793; Archibald 1801; Christian 1803; Allan 1804; Mary 1806; John 1809.

McLean, John (< 1765) m. **Mary Paterson** in Aintuim on 1st Jan. 1788; 8 bpts. in **KLN OPR**. Allan in Aintuim, 1788; Ann in Aintuim 1793; Donald in Mingary 1796; Mary in Mingary 1798; Lauchlan n.p. 1802; Lauchlan in Dervaig 1805; Catherine in Kilmore 1806; Lachlan in Mingary 1810.

McLean, John (c.1773->1851) schoolmaster m. **Margaret McCallum** 26 Jan. 1802 'publickly' **KLN OPR**. Bpts. at Balligown [Torloisk estate]: Alexander 7 Nov. 1802; Archibald 30 Mar. 1806;

John 30 Oct. 1808; Lachlan 16 Sep. 1810; Flora 21 Dec. 1812; Margaret 2 Apr. 1815; Mary 20 Jan. 1817; Jane 25 May 1820. The death of Elizabeth McLean aged 83 in Tobermory 1890 gives these parents' names, but only likely date for her birth is 1804. Another puzzle is a chatty entry in OPR 13 Oct. 1805: "*John McLean, schoolmaster became sponsor for, and obtained Baptism to the Natural son of Marey his dau.r. not acknowledged by the alledged Father – the child's name is Archibald. Against the baptism Archibald McColl Merchant protested, and took instruments in the Beadle's hands.*" If John was b. c.1773, and had a dau. of childbearing age in 1805, this Marey must have been his nat. dau., and both f. and dau. must have procreated at a very young age. In **CEN KLN 1841** John is 68, his w. 62, Alexander 32, John 26, Margaret 22 and Jane 18. In 1851 John is 65 [75?] Margaret 75, Alexander still unm. 48, John unm. 40, Jane unm. 30, and 2 gr.-sons are 'scholars' – Neil McLean 14 and John McLean 11. In 1861 John and Margaret are gone, Archibald is head, unm.42 [b. 1806] and his siblings have impossible ages – Jane 28, John 40. A nephew Donald McLean 14 is a 'scholar', and there are 2 nieces, Margaret McInnes, 16 and Margaret McKinnon 14. The schoolmaster's sons are referred to in a letter of 12 Feb. 1836 from Alexander Shiells to Mrs Clephane **JC/MIP p.183** "*John McLean the schoolmaster's two sons , Alexander & John were the worst [for fighting at funerals] but specially John. They both struck a strong lad who never struck them in return…*" See McLean, Alexander (1802-1860), his s., and McLean, Elizabeth (1804?-1890) his dau. The dau. Mary bpt. in 1817 seems to be living next door in 1861 aged 36, with ch. Mary McInnes 13, John McInnes 11, Jane McInnes 3. **JC/MIP**

McLean, John (c.1777-1860s) m. **Flory McLeod**, dau. of Donald McLeod & Margaret Rankin 30 Jan. 1812 (but careful here, as another couple with exactly the same names m. 23 Jan.1807, so that it is difficult to distinguish bpts. for these 2 couples). This couple were in Dervaig and the other in Penmore, but this John moved to Drimnacroish c.1822 and was still there in 1851 when he was 74, Flory 55. [A Flory was actually bpt. to Donald & Margaret in 1791, but her age was always given out as b.c.1795, and perhaps she was!] These are the parents of Hector (1813-1896), John (b.1814), Betty (b.1817 and called after her gr.-mo. Elizabeth McLachlan), Mary (b.1820), Lachlan (b.1822), Donald (b.1823),

Catherine (b.1826) and Peter b. c.1828-30. In **CEN KLN 1861** Drimnacroish, John & Flory's ages have jumped to 88 and 74, and John's b.p. is Sunipol. Flory McLeod d. a wid. at Dervaig 1880 aged 88.

McLean, John (b.1781- d. in 1850s) miller in Penmore KLN – one of the great family of Penmore McLean millers, he m. **Catherine McKinnon**, 10 years his junior. Bpts. in KLN OPR are John (q.v.) 1815, Alexander (q.v.) 1817, Catherine 1821, Margaret 1823, twins Neil & Hugh (q.v.) 1826. Others lost in KG have been re-constructed as Donald c.1830, Lachlan c.1833, Mary c.1836, Janet 1838. In **CEN KLN 1851** with w. Catherine & ch. John 35, Alexander33, Catherine 29, Margaret 27, Donald 23, Mary 19, Janet 13. In **CEN KLN 1861** his s. John aged 45, has replaced him as miller with his w., Catherine [McMaster] 30 (b. Ardnamurchan). Catherine McKinnon 70, is a wid. in household. She d. at Penmore in 1880. Her parents were Neil McKinnon & Flora Morison.

McLean, John (c.1781) tenant in Suie KLF he m. (1) **Elizabeth McLaine** 3 Apr. 1806. Ch. in **KLF OPR** were John, Ann, Allan, Archibald [bpt. Sep. 1815 > his mo.'s death]; m. (2) **Isabella Cameron** from Knocknafenaig 25 Mar. 1817. 2nd family Archibald 1818, Elizabeth 1820, Alexander 1825, Marion 1827, Archibald 1830, Marion 1832, Ann 1834. In **CEN KLF 1841** Ardtun he is 60 with w. Bell 45, John, Alexander & Elizabeth. Isabella Cameron d. 1879 in Canada; bur. Port Elgin, Ont.

McLean, John (c.1781-1859) tailors. of John McLean post & Chirsty McLean, he d. a wid. 1859 at Portonan, Torosay, aged 78. In CEN TRS 1851 at Portonan (Grasspoint) John McLean is 73, pauper, "Old Postman" with s. Alexander 17, shoemaker.

McLean, John (c.1782-1864) s. of Charles McLean, cottar & Margaret Campbell pauper, formerly fisherman, he d. 15 Mar. 1864 at Ardtun aged 82 of cerebral apoplexy. **CEN KLF 1861** Ardtun has John McLean 80, fisherman, pauper, b. KLF with **Julian [Mitchell]** w. 60, Mary McDougall, dau. m. 27, Alexander McDougall s.-in-law, m. 28, quarrier, and Robina Bell, gr-dau. 7, scholar. John & Julian had had at least 11 ch. from 1820 in **KLF OPR**, and lived at Garacreich, Ardtun. Julian was b. Coll. Their dau. Marion m. William Reid, quarrier at Ardfenaig [Camas] in **CEN KLF 1851**, when John's sons, Lachlan 28 & Charles 20 were also quarriers, living with

William Reid at Camas.

McLean, John (1784-1867) 1 of the many Torloisk estate Macleans who slipped off quietly to Canada in the 1820s. He m. Flory McInnes in Fanmore KLN 30 July 1816; Alexander was bpt. 19 Oct. 1817, Flory 29 Aug. 1819. A couple of exactly the same names now began to have ch. in Sorn KLN – Margaret 21 Sep. 1823, Neil 27 Nov. 1825, but because of GK it is difficult to know if they are different people. John & Flory may have been evicted from Tostary c.1820 when Mrs Maclean Clephane was cutting down on dependants. John is said to be a s. of Lauchlan McLean & Christian McMillan who had been m. 12 Dec. 1777, and who lived in Ensay, but some sources say that Christian's name was Mary. Whatever the case may be, a family with these names went to Canada, where some are bur. at MacMillan Cemetery, Osnabruck Township, Stormont Co., Ontario.

McLean, John (<1785) shoemaker in Tobermory in the Breast or Shore Street, he m. **Marion or Sarah Livingston** 1 Feb. 1816; ch. in **KLN OPR & SLN & TBR Mission** are Catherine 27 Jan. 1817, Abraham (q.v.) 30 Jan. 1819, James 3 Dec. 1822 & Sarah 12 Feb. 1825. In **CEN TBR 1851** John is 68 with Sarah 61, Donald s. unm. 21, Sarah unm. 27, Grace dau. unm. 19.

McLean, John (c.1785-1863) vintner, Portmore, TBR , s. of Malcolm McLean feuar & Chirsty Lamont, he m. **Catherine Johnstone** who predeceased him. He d. 22 Apr. 1863 aged 78 of gravel from info of Murdoch Kennedy, master mariner, s.-in-law, residing at Portmore. JM is in 1861 census at Portmore Public House, wid., 80, public house keeper, b. Coll (but in **CEN 1851** he was b. TBR) in 5 rooms, with Betty McDonald gr.-dau. 14, dom. servt. In same census at'Kennedy's' Ann Kennedy marr. 40, captain's w., b. Tiree in 5 rooms must be John's dau. She has Catherine dau. 11, 'scholar' b. Tobermory & Mary McLean visitor, 35, servt. b. Ardnamurchan. There are 2 bpts. in **KLN OPR** for John McLean & Catherine Johnstone in Achnasaul: Flory 15 Aug. 1824 & Lachlan 20 Aug. 1826. Any others will be unrecorded because of the GK. The other ch. are in **CEN TBR 1841**, Portmore when John is 50, publican, Catherine 40, Ann 20, Flory 15, Lachlan 13, Ketty 12, Donald 10 & Robert 6. Donald & Robert were bakers in **CEN TBR 1851**. Robert d. TBR 1855 aged 18. Lachlan emig. to Canada with Maclean cousins, and this emig.is recorded in

McLean, John (c.1790) farmer in Penmore, m. to a **Peggy**. Their first s. in **CEN 1841** was Kenneth b. c.1824. In 1841 John was 45, Peggy 40, Kenneth 15; Ann 14; Jessie 12; John 8; Hugh 6; Alexander 4; Archibald 2. In **CEN 1851** JM 60, Peggy 58; Catherine Fletcher dau. m. 29; Kenneth McLean s. m. 27 boatman; Hugh McLean s. 17; Alexander McLean, s.14; Archd. McPhaden servt. 15; Jane McLean s.'s dau. 6 mo. Donald McDonald visitor Unm. 40 sailor. In **CEN KLN 1861** Farm of Aird, JM 65 farmer, Peggy 62; Alexander s. unm. 23;Ann McLean niece 5; Isabella Campbell servt. unm. 18 – all b. KLN.

McLean, John (<1790) carpenter in Greenock in c.1841, s. of Hector McLean in Glenbyre and Flora McLean, gr.-s. of Neil McLean in Fishnish & [?] McDougall. He was one of the beneficiaries in the Will of Miss Mary McLean, matron of the Town's Hospital in Glasgow who d. 1834.

McLaine, John (c.1790-1825) On 1 May 1815, John McLaine & **Helen McLaine** in Fishnish TRS were m., and on the same day had their last. dau. Anne bpt. and legitimised by their marr. Yet in Nov. of the same year in **TRS OPR** a 'child in fornication' is recorded as Alexander, presumably because he was conceived out of wedlock and when Nelly was still in Corrynachenchy. Archibald was bpt. 1817, John 1824, and on 28 May 1825, Lauchlan Maclaine (q.v.) the diarist notes the death from consumption of John McLaine at Fishnish *"leaving a widowed mother childless and a young weak family of four orphans, 2 boys & 2 girls."* For the sequel, See McLean, Ann (bpt. 1815) his dau.

McLaine, John (c.1791-1856) weaver in Croggan, s. of Charles McLaine (q.v. – spelt McLean) farmer & Sarah Currie, he m. 22 Nov. 1814, **Catherine Livingston** when both in Moy. Recorded ch. in OPR TRS at Moy were Donald 1817, Margaret 1819, Jean 1821, Charles 1823, Hector 1825, but there were others, incl. John c.1830. In 1851 his sons Donald and John were fishermen, still unm. and living at home. John d. 11 May 1856 aged 65 In 1861 Catherine, widowed, shared her croft at Croggan with John, and her s.-in-law Duncan McFarlane, who had m. her dau. Margaret McLaine. The McFarlanes had 5 ch. in 1861. In 1881, Catherine Livingstone was still going strong aged 81 at Barnashoig with s. John 37, his w. Mary 26, & her gr.-dau. Catherine 2. She d. aged 84 in 1875, when her parents' names were given as Donald Livingston & Euphemia Campbell, who had been 18th C. LB tenants at Moy & Cameron.

McLaine, John (c.1791) in Ledirkle TRS he m. 12 July 1827 **Ann Cameron**, also from Ledirkle. Bpts in TRS OPR: Hector 1828, Donald 1830, Mary 1833. In **LMD/Souls** 1829 at Ledirkle John is 38 with 'Mrs' 24 but no ch. Hector. The Cameron family was close by. In **CEN TRS 1841** they are still at Ledirkle, John 50 being a tenant, Ann 30, Hector 12, Donald 10, Mary 8, Neil 6, Catherine 2. John McLaine is frequently referred to in **LMD**, but there were several in this small area of similar age.

McLean, John (c.1800) crofter in Kingharair, a traditional breeding-ground of McLeans in valley of the R. Bellart, KLN and part of Torloisk estate. There are no bpts. or marr. for this man because of GK, but his w. was a **Flora** and reconstructed ch. Mary or Marion c.1835, Sandy c.1837, Flora c. 1839, Hector c.1841, Catherine c.1845, Charles c. 1850, Jane c.1853. But in 1871 we find the mo. a pauper 64, with her s. Charles 19, also a pauper [suggesting he had an infirmity, as healthy young men were not admitted to the Poor Roll] and in that 1-roomed 'pauper house' 2 gr-ch. Mary & Ronald McLean, 12 and 5. **CEN KLN 1851, 1861, 1871**

McLean, John (c.1802-1875) lab. single, s. of John McLean farmer & Peggy McCallum, he d. aged 65 at Portmore, TBR of erysipelas of right arm, 1875 aged 65, his sister Jane McLean being present.

McLean, John (1805) shepherd bpt. 27 Oct.1805 s. of Alexander McLean & Marion McLean, then in Stronbuy, but his mo. was in Sunipol at the time of her marr. 1804. She d. a wid. in 1861 at Torasa-Quinish aged 79. John was 1st of 8 ch. in **KLN OPR**. He m. **Anne McArthur**, was in Torasa-Quinish in **CEN KLN 1851** as a shepherd aged 45 with Anne 40, Catherine 15, John 11, Alexander 10, Hector 8, Lachlan, 5, Hugh 3 and Euphemia 6 mos. His mo. Marion, 65, lived next door, and this census reveals she was b. in Coll. John remained in Torasa-Quinish in **CEN KLN 1861** and Drimnacroish in 1871 & 1881. His w. Anne also known as Agnes was 71 in **CEN KLN 1881**,when John was 75. See McLean, Hector (c.1843-1915) their s.

McLean, John (c.1814) b. in Salen area, he m. a **Cirsty** c.1844 and was living in Crogan in **CEN KLS 1851** aged 37 with his w. 35, Margaret 6,

Charles 4, Sarah 1 and his bro. Donald 30. This leads us perhaps to identify him as JM husband of Cirsty McLaine at Drimnatyne, KLS. In 1871 a 'common labourer' in Crogan Village aged 36 and b. Pennygown is too young, yet has a w. Cirsty 33, and s. Allan 16.

McLean, John (b.c.1815) shoemaker in **CEN TBR 1851** at Portmore, with w. **Mary** 35, b. Tiree, dau. Nancy 7, Mary 5, b. Tiree; Flora 3 & Donald 1 both b. Kilmore.

McLean, John (bpt.1815) miller s. of John McLean (q.v.) miller in Penmore & and Cate McKinnon, he was 35 and a joiner in **CEN KLN 1851** Penmore in house of his parents, with his w. **Catherine** [**McMaster** m. 31 Aug. 1847] & ch., Hugh c.1849, Christina c.1850. In 1861 he has added Archibald 7,Margaret 5, Alexander 3, Catherine 1 (q.v. – accidentally drowned shortly after the census) his mo. Catherine 70 a wid. In 1871 he is a crofter in Penmore with w. and Hugh 21, Christina Ann 19, Margaret 14, Alexander 12, Dugald 8, Catherine 6 and John 3. His mo., still with them, is now said to be 98, but this is exaggerated. Cate McKinnon d. in 1880 aged 88. In 1881, in a remarkable survival, aged 60, he has been promoted to 'farmer' of 75 acres, with his w. and Flora, Dugald, Margaret, Catherine, John still at home.

Maclaine, John Campbell (1818-1885) 3rd s. of Murdoch Maclaine 20th of LB, he went to Java, then to NZ & Australia, employed at Tahara Sheep Station as a book-keeper latterly. A report in the *Western Agriculturalist* of 6 Dec. 1884 of his last days: "*Mr J. Maclaine. book-keeper at Tahara Station…had spent all the evening in Coleraine and mounted his horse in the yard of Trathor's Koroite Inn for the purpose of returning to the Station… the horse appears to be restive and commenced bucking … before getting out of the yard threw his rider heavily, Mr Maclaine falling on his head… stunned by the blow… .*" He was apparently unm.

McLean, John (c.1829-1893) proprietor of Gometra with his bro. Peter, he d. unm. less than 3 mos. <him. A nephew, John Morrison gave info. See McLean, Hector (1772-1846) his f.

McLean, John (c.1826-1876) sailor s. of George McLean farmer & Cirsty McDonald, m. to **Ann Cameron**, he d. at Burg, KLN 1876, in presence of his nephew George McLean.

Maclean, John Ralph (1827-1903) "*the only*

representative of the Uisken family now living" according to **AMS/CG** in 1899,he d. of acute pneumonia, a mercantile clerk, unm., 28 Apr. 1903 at 4 Govanhill Street, Glasgow, aged 71. His f. was Archibald Maclean Lieut. 56th Foot, his mo. Marion Maclean M/S McPherson. The info at death was given by a 2nd cousin named McPherson. John Ralph at one time studied medicine, matriculating at Glasg. Univ. under the plain name of John Maclean in 1846. He was 1 of the group of relatives who contested the Will of Lieut.-Col. Alexander Maclean, his uncle (1777-1859). See **JC/MIP**. He had 2 sisters, Lilias (b.1823) & Margaret Alicia. His own dates were 1827-1903, so cousin's info was incorrect. But parents' names accurate. His mo., Marion came from Lagganulva.

McLean, John (c.1830-1893) bro. of Donald & Peter McLean (q.v.), proprietors of Ulva, s. of Hector McLean (q.v.) & Flora McArthur in Kingharair, he d. single at Gometra 17 Feb. 1893, his nephew John Morrison being with him at his death.

McLean, John (1835-1855) b. Reudle, s. of Charles McLean tailor & Mary Livingston, he d. aged 19, KLN 1855.

McLean, John (c.1838) seaman in Dervaig m. in Glasgow 24 Mar.1865 **Margaret McFadyen**, who already had a dau., Christina McLean. In **CEN KLN 1871** John is 33, Margaret 32, Mary Ann 5, Flora 3, John A. McLean 1.

McLean, John (1851-1909) mercht. at Dervaig. See entry for Hector McLean (1813-1896) his f., and GRV for Catherine McDonald, his mo., in Kilmore. He m. **Helen Beaton** (c.1864-1915). John was postmaster, 24, in **CEN KLN 1881** Dervaig; he d. New Year's Eve 1909 at Dervaig aged 58 of epilepsy, John Beaton his bro.-in-law giving info.

Mclean, Julian (<1748) dau. of a nat. s. of Donald 3rd of Brolass, James McLean, who was killed in America, & his w. Julia dau. of Allan McLean of Garmony, f. of John Maclaine 17th of LB. Julian was thus a niece both of John Lochbuy & his w. 'Lady Lochbuy', as well as of Sir Allan, 'the Knight'. She m. 1764, Duncan McPhaden, tenant in Garmony, s. of Gilbert McPhaden, being well-connected enough to have a marr. contract. **GRO**

Maclaine, Julian (1775-1840) dau. of Gillean Maclaine (q.v.) of Scallastle, she nearly m. John

Gregorson of Ardtornish in 1797, but was prevented by her mo. Marie McQuarrie, at which "*Julianna was amazing angry…*" On the rebound she m. Collector [of Customs] **Thomas Ross** when he was stationed in Tobermory. 2 sons, Archibald and Murdoch John were b. at Ledirkle in Mull before the couple moved on to Oban and Ayr. Thomas was alive after his wife's death. There was another s. Daniel, who wrote 22 Feb. 1821 to his uncle, "*I am now God be thanked, going out to New South Wales under the auspices of Sir Thomas Brisbane, the recently appointed Governor, who has promised to do for me when I get out there… and has also promised me a large grant of land. I have wrote to Col. Macquarie to see if he can give me an introduction to his brother the General…*" The couple also had a dau. Mary Ross, who had a literary reputation as a writer and collector of poetry. Julian is said to have been 'vile' and 'drunken'. **GRO/Glouc./LMD**

McLean, Julian (c.1784-1862) dau. of Hector McLean & Flora Brown, in Fidden, she m. **Angus McPhail**, herd, 11 Feb. 1812, and had a s. Hector in 1813. But bpt. of Flora in 1816 indicates that Julian is already a wid. It is not certain that either of her ch. survived, for she appears alone in **CEN KLF 1841** at Toatbhreac under her M/S in household of her nephew Dugald McPhee, and was there also in 1851, and d. aged 78 from a malignant tumour in the groin.

McLean, Julian Ann (1797-1874) unm. sister of Alexander Maclean of Pennycross, 'Sandy PX', dau. of Archibald of PX & Alice Maclean, she d. aged 77, 14 Dec. 1874 at Carsaig, from congestion of lungs.

McLean, Kenneth (b. c.1824) in **CEN KLN 1841** in household of his f. John McLean farmer, 45 and his mo. Peggy 40 he is 15 with siblings Ann 14, Jessie 12, John 8, Hugh 6, Alexander 4, Archibald 2. On 16 Jun.1849, he m. in Glasgow, **Isabella McLean**. In **CEN KLN 1851** at his f.'s house, he is 27, m. to Isabella 22 and with dau. Jane McLean 6 mos. It may be Kenneth who went to Finch Ontario c.1857 and returned to Mull c.1863. In 1868, Kenneth McLean Boatman in Tobermory and Isabel McLean, M/S McLean, had a s. Hector. In **CEN TBR 1871** Isabella is m. 40, with Eliza 16, Hugh 15, John 14 – all b. Penmore, but Margaret dau. 12 'scholar' b. FINCH, ONTARIO; Isabella 8, scholar, b. Penmore; Hugh 6 scholar, b. Tobermory; Hector 3 b. Tobermory. It looks as if this family emigrated to Ontario and returned to Mull.

Maclaine, Kenneth Douglas Lorne (1880-1935) b. in London. From a roly-poly baby in **CEN KLS 1881** (see Murdoch Gillean, his f.) K.D.L. Maclaine was to grow to succeed in 1910 as Maclaine of Lochbuy, or 'Lochbuie' as it had come to be called. He went on the stage, touring US & Canada as a Gaelic & English singer. Whilst he served in WW1, LB was let to Sir Stephen Herbert Gatty, who, in a complex arrangement had also lent money to KDLM, on which interest was to be paid at set intervals. In those days before bankers' orders, the payer had to remember to send a cheque by post, but in the mitigating circumstances of wartime, both KDLM & his mother were unable to supply one of the payments *punctually*, upon which failure Sir Stephen called in the forces of the law and demanded his pound of flesh – the collateral – which was the estate of Lochbuy. An almost farcical appeal in the House of Lords revolved round the precise meaning of the word *punctual* with reference to a payment. The appeal failed, and Lochbuy was lost, but with the death of Sir Stephen Gatty in 1922 the estate was sold to a new buyer. KDLM had m. at the height of his misfortune in 1920, Olive Stewart-Richardson, who should be gratefully acknowledged as the lady responsible for depositing the fabulous MS collection of Lochbuy Papers in **NAS**

Maclean, Lachlan (1720-1799) 7th of Torloisk. 2nd s. of Donald Torloisk, he inherited the estate in 1765 after the death of his sardonic bro, Hector (q.v.) who, with his other bro. Allan, had mocked Lachlan's lifestyle in letters. *"…one of the honestest & best men in the world, but will never make anything of this world – will never be rich – honest heart, good soul – the wife still not with child …"* and *"Brother Lauchlan is pretty well in health but is the same man – just as easily imposed upon by the World as ever…"* Lachlan had a trading ship, and was reluctant to retire to Torloisk. He had m. c.1762, **Margaret Smith**, a lady of refinement, who after the birth of 1 dau., Marianne (q.v.), retired from childbearing. No sooner had he taken on Torloisk than all his siblings in concert sued him for the sums the estate owed them. He quickly learned to distrust his bro. Allan and all relations, inviting foreigners to sumptuous spreads at Torloisk, and treating his family frugally. Other heritors were not allowed to treat with him in their wonted style. He charged Murdoch LB 8 years' interest on a pair of

millstones bought in 1790 and unpaid in 1898. He built a new house c. 1782 on 'Lethir Baile Neil' then 'without trees or verdure', and made Marianne his heir, but lived to see her produce no sons. **JC/MIP**

McLean, Lachlan (<1730->1781) schoolmaster in Pennygown who taught Mally Maclaine (q.v.) Lauchlan Maclaine & his half-bro. Allan Maclaine Scallastle, for whom Gillean Maclaine had to pay £6 each yearly in 1781. Prob. employed by the SSPCK as parish teacher, and for a time at the *Schola Illustris* at Aros, where Latin, Greek & Mathematics were taught. **JC/MIP**

McLean, Lachlan Ban (1751-1819) innkeeper Bunessan, served in the army with Sir Allan Maclean (q.v.) but returned to Mull before 1773 to run the Inn which still survives as the Argyll Arms. In **ERC/Inhabitants 1779** he is change keeper aged 28, already with a w., **Mary McLean** of Torran, 2 sons (Allan 7, John 4) 2 daus. 2 other sons, Hector Hugh (q.v.) and Charles (an army surgeon who m. Lucy Quinn, Dublin in 1837) came later. His daus. were Sibella, Mary, Catherine and Isabel. They m. respectively, Adjutant McCallum, Allan McLean (q.v.), John McCallum and Capt. Duncan Campbell (d.1834) of the 91st Regt. His s. John, 'John Bunessan' continued as innkeeper, and agent for Lloyds shipping insurance in Mull, but was unm. and known to be paralysed in 1831.

McLean, Lauchlan (<1760) m. 27 Mar. 1781 when at Laggan, KLN, **Mary McDougall**. Bpts. in **KLN OPR** at Laggan & Kilbrenan were Alexander 25 Nov. 1781, Flora 1786, Neil 1789, Allan 1790, Hector 1794, Hugh 1795, Janet 1797. Nothing else is heard of them.

McLean, Lachlan (<1760) 'Lachlan Dantzig' s. of a tenant in Scallastle part of LB, under jurisdiction of Gillean Maclaine (q.v.) but formerly in Pennygown, and Lachlan appears to have had an excellent education at Pennygown or Aros, which enabled him to go into trade in Dublin & Dantzig. His f. un-named d. Jul. 1781. There was a step-mo. and poss. a half-bro. from 2nd marr. Gillean confided to L. the follies of the laird of LB in running the estate, and adventures of Archy LB. Marie, Gillean's w. wrote in 1781: *"I am told Lauchlan Dancike is in a very bad steat of helth since he went home. Let me now how his stepmother is when you write me nixt…"* **NAS GD174/1337**

McLean, Lauchlan (<1770) soldier in the

fencibles, he came from Drimnacroish KLN on his marr. to **Mary McNiven** 8 Feb. 1791, bpts. reflecting his absence on service – Duncan 22 Dec. 1791, Catherine 1794, Mary 1800, Christian 1802, Mairon 1804, Anne 1806.

McLean, Lauchlan (<1770) with w. **Mary McLean** he was in Balligown, KLN from c. 1800 with ch. Patrick 1801, Neil 1803, John 1806, Margaret 1808, Marion 1811, John 1813, Neil 1816, Jean 1819, and possibly Mary McLean, 80, wid. in 1851 with unm. s. John 35 & marr. dau. Jane McDonald 29 is the remnant of this family.

McLean, Lauchlan (<1770) a remarkable number of McLean families multiply in 1800-1820 on the Torloisk estate, and disappear, giving rise to the suspicion that Mrs Maclean Clephane was weeding out those who did not pay rent arrears. A proliferation of Lauchlans in this area makes it difficult to distinguish families. Many were given the name in honour of Lachlan Maclean (q.v.) of Torloisk, their laird from 1765-1799. This Lauchlan, like the one above, with his w. **Margaret Shaw** had Flora 1802, John 1804, Neil & Catherine 1806, Jean 1812, Allan 1814, Allan 1815, Mary 1816, seem to vanish without trace.

Maclaine, Lauchlan (1771-1847) diarist, 'LMD' nat. s. of Gillean Maclaine & Janet McPhail, he was b. Edinburgh 9 Jun. 1771, 3 wks. < his f. m. Marie McQuarrie, dau. of Lachlan McQuarrie of Ulva; brought up and educated by his f., who had himself been a nat. s. of John Maclaine of LB. Sent to Jamaica in 1789, he returned to Mull in 1813-15, went back to Jamaica, and retired c.1821 to a humble house which he rented at Garmony. From 1815 he wrote a diary daily, the section from 1824-1836 written about his life in Mull and the people in the area around Fishnish, Garmony, Scallastle, Corrynachenachy, Ledirkle, and the hamlet of Craignure which barely existed < 1836. As an observer with a foot in each camp – 'gentles' and 'commoners', his observations on lairds of LB & Achnacroish (now Torosay Castle), on ministers, and on privations & shortcomings of the cottars, are invaluable. He d. Oban 1847. **JC/MIP; GRO LMD**

McLean, Lachlan (b.1774) prob. the boy in **ERC/Inhabitants** 1779 aged 5 at Acharn, s. of John McLean tenant there aged 50 in 1779. He m. **Catherine McLean** 30 May 1797. Baptisms: Duncan (q.v.) 1801, Ann 11803, Donald 1805, Allan 1808, Flory 1815. He had a bro. Allan b.

c.1765 & bro. Charles b. c.1769.

McLean, Lachlan (c.1774-1860) crofter s. of Hugh McLean & Anne Brown, m. **Flory Rankin**, d. 19 Apr. 1860 at Penmore aged 86 of the infirmities of Old Age. Bur. Calgary. IN **CEN KLN 1851** at Penmore, Lachlan was b. ARD, his w. in MRV. They had been in Mull since < 1818. They had Morison gr.-ch. – hence the Rankin-Morison connection. Flora Rankin d. in 1861 aged 83, dau. of Hugh Rankin, miller & Mary Rankin, M/S Rankin. Known ch. were Bell, Mary & John.

McLean, Lauchlan (<1775) m. 13 Oct. 1795, **Mary McPhaiden** when they were in Penmollach, Quinish, KLN. They had Allan bpt. 10 Dec. 1795, Flora 1797, Fflora 1802 (in Achnasaul, nearby) Winifred 1807, Hector 1808, Anne 1810, Ann 1812 all in Dervaig. **CRD** of Allan McLean (q.v.) aged 57 at Croig Inn on 13 Dec. 1855 may not accurately reflect his age, but shows that these McLeans did not emigrate.

McLean, Lachlan (<1778) m. **Janet Cameron** <1798, lived at Kilmore KLN. 4 daus. in OPR, Janet, Mary, John & Flora (q.v. 1805-1863).

Maclaine, Lachlan (c.1780-1843) shoemaker of the Paisley family who worried the Maclaines of Lochbuy with their possibly greater claim to the estate of LB by being descended from a s. of Lachlan Mor of LB who had d. c.1684. He was s. of Allan Maclaine who had enjoyed farms in Scallastle passed down from his gr.f. Allan Maclaine, who had been in fact an illegit. s. of Lachlan Mor. He m. Mary Cameron in Renfrew 24 Feb. 1804, and was f. of Allan Maclaine (q.v. 1814-1881).

McLean, Lauchlan (<1784) another vanishing Lauchlan, he was in Mingary KLN on his marr. to **Mary McArthur**, Burg, in Feb. 1805, settled in Balligown (Torloisk estate), bpt. Flora 1810, Hugh 1813, Mary 1815 & Donald 1818.

McLean, Lachlan (c.1784-1855) m. **Sarah McGillivray**. **GRV** at Knock, KLN, says "*In memory of Lachlan Maclean who died at Torloisk 11 April 1855 aged 70 years and 9 months; also his wife Sarah McGilvray aged 72 years. Erected by their sons Charles and Angus.*"

McLean, Lachlan (b.c.1790?) m. **Ann McLean**, was tenant in Tapull [Tavool] & Scobull [L.Scridain], he was 50 in **CEN KLF 1841** at 'Scoble', and a farmer, with his w. Ann 40, his daus. Helen 20, Mary 15, Catherine 12, and sons Neil 10, John 8, Donald 6. It appears from the documentation of the executry of Miss Mary McLean, matron of the Town's Hospital, Glasgow, who d. 1834, that he was the bro. of Charles, Neil, Ann and Catherine McLean, who were all, like him, beneficiaries of their cousin's estate. He was therefore the s. of Duncan & Mary McLeans, and gr.s. of Neil McLean in Fishnish. Lachlan and Neil had both left Ardmeanach by 1851. See McLean, Mary (d.1834) and **JC/MIP** for an account of the sales of Ardmeanach. **NAS/GD174/268** for McLean genealogy.

McLean, Lachlan (c.1793-1850s) farmer in Fanmore, KLN, he m. **Flora** < 1829, so all his ch. are in GK., and have to be re-constructed from censuses: Mary c.1829, Donald c.1832, Lachlan c.1835, John c.1837, Hector c.1839, Charles & Ann c.1841, Peter c. 1844. Lachlan McLean is 58 in **CEN 1851** at Fanmore, but dead by 1861, when Flora is a crofting wid. 54 at Fanmore with Donald, Lachlan & Hector, all helping.

McLean, Lachlan (<1795) another McLean-McGilvra marr. was at Ardtun, KLF, 19 May 1818. The Bunessan weaver was poss. much older than his w., and it is tempting to think she might be the servant girl, Catherine McGilvra, who had borne a s. to Hector Hugh Maclean (q.v.) only a short time before. A dau. of Donald McGilvra, crofter & Janet Beaton, she bore Lachlan between 1819 and 1835, 5 girls in succession – Marion, Margaret, Janet, Flora, Catherine, then Charles, Donald and John, the last. Lachlan prob. d. c.1835-7. She was in Ardtun with her 4 youngest ch. in 1841. Her dau. Margaret m. Donald Cameron; her dau. Catherine m. Thomas Rae. **Catherine McGilvra** d. at Lee, Ardtun 8 Mar. 1889 aged 94.

McLean, Lachlan (c.1798-1870) cottar at Aird of Kinloch, m. to **Mary McDonald**, dau. of Finlay McDonald & Catherine McLean. 1 dau. in records, Ann, bpt. at Kinloch 8 Oct. 1832. In 1851 Lachlan 53, Mary 55 & Ann 20 are at Kinlochscridain KLF. Mary McDonald d.at Kinloch 7 Feb.1865 aged 70. Lachlan d. a wid. in 1870 aged 68. His parents were Hector McLean crofter & Anne McLean M/S McLean.

McLean, Lachlan (c.1800-1870s) small tenant at Scobul m. to **Catherine McMillan**. From 1851 the family was on the Poor Roll, when Lachlan was 51, Catherine 48, Donald 17, Janet 15. Catherine & her unm. sister Mary were daus. of Rory McMillan the miller & Mary McLean. See **JC/MIP** p.271. Catherine d. at Scobul, a wid.

aged 82 in 1883.

McLean, Lachlan (c.1810) crofter in Dervaig m. to **Marion McDonald** in **CEN KLN 1841** & **1851**. From these their ch. can be construed as being b. 1830-45 – Lachlan, Magnus (q.v.), Mary, Donald, Hector (q.v.). Marion's sister Bell McDonald lives with them. The 2 sisters were b. in Arnabost, Coll, Lachlan in Kilbeg KLN. Marion McDonald was dec. at time of her s. Magnus's marr. 1867.

McLean, Lachlan (<1815) in **CEN KLF 1851** the enumerator has volunteered the remark "*that was at service in Glasgow*" about Lachlan to identify husb. of 34-year-old **Flora McLean** at Killunaig Farm. Their ch. were James 13, Donald 10, Nicol 8, Allan 6, Hector 4, John 2. The fact that all they were b. in KLF points again to Killunaig as a black spot for registration, due to its indubitable FC inclinations, for there are no bpts. for this family in **KLF OPR**.

McLean, Lachlan Allan (1820-1864) s. of Capt. Hector McLean, gr. s. of Lachlan Ban Maclean, Bunessan. Bpt. 24 May 1820 at Bunessan, lived in Carsaig. His mo. was Ann Macleod, dau. of Mr Neil Macleod, min. of KLF. He went to America in 1842; fought in Confederate Army. In 1864 he was stabbed and killed in his office at Lexington, Missouri. There is new info in 2000 as he kept a diary which survives. He had m. Eliza Smith in USA and had 1 son, Nelson Robert Maclean.

Maclaine, Lachlan (c.1822) ploughman, b. TRS, m. 1853 at Assapol **Janet Maclaine** b. KLF. They are in **CEN TRS 1871** & **1881** Tiroran, KLF, b. c. 1822 & 1831 with Helen c.1857, Rosa 1864, Gillean c.1869 & a visiting Gillean McKinnon 18 'scholar'.

McLean, Lachlan (bpt.1826) s. of Archibald McLean (q.v.) & Christina McEachern, Ardchiavaig. Living in Glasgow in 1865-71.

McLean, Lachlan (c.1830)master house carpenter employing 1 journeyman and 1 boy, this was an unusually skilled man to be in Bunessan. His 4-roomed house, large by any standards, sheltered his w. and 6 ch. in **CEN KLF 1871**. His w. was a **Mary** 36, and his ch. b. in different places – Charles in Glasgow c.1857, Hugh in Kildalton (Islay) c.1859, Margaret in Glasgow c.1863, Mary in KLF c.1865.

McLean, Lachlan (c.1833-1892) crofter & postman, s. of Duncan McLean (q.v.) crofter & Ann McLean, M/S McLean. In MEMORIES OF

MULL, Iona McVean describes Lachlan: *"When we first came to Kilfinichen, the 'Old Post' Lachlan McLean walked all the way from Pennyghael to Gribun and back again three days a week – about twenty-six miles or even more. When he arrived at Kilfinichen he used to walk into the kitchen, throw his mail bags in the middle of the floor, and go and sit down by the fire with a book which he produced out of his pocket while we all turned the bags upside down on the floor and hunted through them for our own letters... He didn't take the least notice of all this, but just went steadily on with his book, and I think he always had a cup of tea and something to eat. He was a great reader, and such a nice man. When he died, his two daughters carried on instead, and worked with the mail just as their father had done. It must have been terribly hard work for them during winter. We felt we were becoming horribly civilized when the mails eventually were brought by dogcart."* Lachlan m. **Catherine McGilvray** in Oban 17 Jun.1869 at the age of 34 in FC. She was 25, from Kinloch KLF, dau. of Archibald McGilvray & Christina McFayden. Lachlan & Catherine had Ann, Christina, Donald & Jessie (both d. of scarlet fever 1887) before she d. at the early age of 37 in 1880. A baby girl of 5 mos., Catherine, d. in 1879. Lachlan d. Kinloch aged 58 in 1892. On giving info at death, his bro. Allan McLean 'signed' with a X demonstrating the differences in education existing in one family.

McLean, Lachlan (1839) b. 16 Sep.1839 s. of Hugh McLean (q.v.) mercht. Iona & Effy McLean. He m. 28 Dec. 1871 **Mary McInnes**. Ch. in **CEN KLF 1881** were Hugh 8, Archibald 6, Peter 5, Margaret 1.

McLean, Lachlan (1847-1897) crofter he m. **Christina McArthur** 10 Aug. 1876. His dau. Catherine m. in 1923 in St. Mary's Cathedral Glasgow, Eric CC Llewellin, Monmouth. Lachlan d. after 2 wks. of pneumonia May 17 1897 at Sligeanach, Iona aged 49. His f. was Hector McLean (q.v.) crofter, his mo. Grace Lamont. Hector his s. was present at death. In **CEN KLF 1901** at Sligeanach Hector 28 was head of household, with mo. Christina 51, sister Ella in her 20s, Mary Ann 16, Maggie 14, Catherine 12, Neil 9.

Maclaine, Lillias (1818-1894), single, d. at Java Lodge 28 Jun. 1894 aged 75, of paralysis, in presence of her sister Mary Ann. She was dau. of Murdoch Maclaine (q.v.) of Lochbuy. and

Christian Maclaine M/S Maclean. Known as Lily, she had had an ode composed by LMD on the occasion of her 1st birthday. Her letters are now in Mull Museum, Tobermory. **GRO/LMD**

McLean, Ludovick (1820) s. of Donald Mclaine, m. Effy Lamont; lived at Crogan TRS.

McLean, Magnus (c.1838-1898) s. of Lachlan McLean (q.v.) & Marion McDonald, his bpt. is lost in GK, but he was 29 and a mercantile clerk on his marr. to Lillias Mackenzie in Edinburgh on 18 Sep. 1867. He returned to Mull, farming at Cuin in **CEN 1881**, when he was 42, Lillias 40, Samuel 12, Marion 10, Magnus 8, Lachlan 6. He d. in Edinburgh as a retired wine mercht. 1898 aged 59, when his s. Magnus was present.

Maclean, Malcolm (fl. 1780s) supposed s. of Sir Allan Maclean (q.v.), mentioned by Archibald McKinnon of Torran as *"the pauper Malcolm Maclean of this parish"* in a letter (1842) to Murdoch Maclaine of LB, requesting support, to which LB replied *"It was a shame for those who talked so much of being related to Sir Allan to allow his grandson to be on the Poor Roll as a pauper."* The parish was KLF, but no Malcolm Maclean appears in **CEN KLF 1841**.

McLean, Malcolm (<1760) feuar in Tobermory, m. **Christina Lamont.** See McLean, John (q.v.), vintner (c.1785-1863), his s., McLean, Alexander (c.1794-1866) his s., McLean, Angus (c.1790-1866) his s., and McLean, Charles (c.1783-1863), his s. In a sasine of 1835, Malcolm disposed and settled a lot of land in Portmore with dwelling houses to his s. Hector, under burden of £20 each to his sons Charles, Murdoch & Alexander, *"with the consent of Christian Lamont, his spouse."* [Argyll Sasines 1835]

McLean, Malcolm (c.1813-1875) b. Lettermore, lobster fisher & cottar in Ensay KLN he m. 1841 in Glasgow **Flory McDougall**. Re-constructed family is Neil c.1845, Hector c.1847, Donald c.1850, Archibald c. 1853, Alexander 1855, Ann c.1860. Malcolm d. at Ensay 5 May 1875 aged 60. He was s. of Neil McLean & Ann McNeill. Flora survived him.

Maclaine, Mally (1740-1831) dau. of Lachlan 15th of LB & Katherine McDougall, brought up by her gr.mo. the widowed Isabel McDougall because her mo. Catherine McDougall had re-married the 'coxcomb' Allan McLean of Kilmory. For the kidnap scene in which Mally and her cattle were removed by John Lochbuy and brought to

LB see **JC/MIP**. She m. Allan Maclean of Drimnin as his 2nd w. and was mo. of Donald Maclean WS (q.v.) and 8 others: Margaret, Sibella, John, Mary, Catherine, Louisa, Caroline & Jane.

McLean, Margaret (c.1752-1789?) w. of **Alexander M**., tacksman of Mingary, she was the dau. of Rev. Hector McLean of Coll & Janet McLean. There is an almost illegible GRV for her in Kilmore burial ground. A bpt. in KLN OPR of her s. Hector 23 Sept. 1789 does not seem to agree with dates on GRV.

McLean, Margaret (18th C.) dau. of Hector McLean in Glenbyre & Flora McLean, gr.dau. of Neil McLean in Fishnish, she m. **Archibald McDougall**, carpenter in Greenock, and as a wid. was one of the beneficiaries of the Will of Miss Mary McLean, matron of the Town's Hospital, Glasgow, who d. 1834.

McLean,Margaret (b.1772 d. <1840 ?) dau. of Lachlan McLean & Ann McLeod in Mingary, she m. **Charles Morrison** <1795 and lived at Bellochroy, producing 8 sons (2 sets of twins) and 3 daus. Her s. Roderick Morrison was a mercht. and publican at Bellochroy (Dervaig) and m. Miss Mary McLean, sister of the Rev. Neil McLean (q.v.)

McLean, Margaret (1776-1813) or Maclaine, dau. of Farquhar Maclaine (q.v.) 'honest Farquhar' & Betty Macquarie, brought up at Oskamull, she m. **John McPherson** Oskamull <1808, with 3 ch. in KLN OPR, Margaret 1809, Charles 1811 and Lachlan McPherson 1813, whose birth cost Margaret her life. "*Elizabeth and I greatly grieved & afflicted to hear of the death of our poor dear niece Margaret... poor dear young creature... her poor aged parents singularly unlucky in their family in thus losing prematurely their two best & favoured daughters*", wrote her uncle, Governor Lachlan Macquarie. Whereabouts of John McPherson and descendants unknown.

McLean, Margaret (c.1784-1876) wid. of **John Graham** crofter, she d. at Ardtun 1876 aged 92, her parents' names being given as Allan McLean cottar & Ann McEachern by her s., Archibald Graham. Since she was b. 20 yrs. <**KLF OPR** began, it is her parents' names that interest us here. There are 5 possible fathers called Allan McLean in **ERC/Inhabitants**.

McLean, Margaret (c.1785-1860) d. Tobermory 1860 see McLean, Peggy (c.1785-1860).

Maclaine, Margaret Ann (1788-1855) 14th and last ch. of Gillean Maclaine & Marie McQuarrie, brought up at Scallastle & Ledirkle, she m. **William Craig** WS, eldest s. of James Craig of the Excise, 9 Dec. 1818. LMD's favourite sister, they carried on a correspondence which survives in **GRO/Glouc**. At William Craig's funeral at West Kirk, Edinburgh [now St Cuthbert's] 7 Jan. 1826, there was a hearse with 4 horses, 5 coaches. No Craig descendants have been discovered so far.

McLean, Margaret Smith (b.c.1795) dau. of John McLean of Langamull (who d. 1810) she m. Lieut. **Simon Fraser** of the 4th West India Regt. of Foot on 1st Dec. 1817. Bpts. to them in KLN OPR [there may have been earlier ones elsewhere] were: Mary McLean Fraser 14 Feb. 1820 at Kingharair; Flora Fraser 31 Jul. 1821 at K; Alexandrina Flora Fraser 23 Feb. 1823 at K; John Fraser 3 Feb. 1827 at K; Elizabeth Harriet Macquarie Fraser 22 Sep. 1832 [called after the w. of Lachlan Macquarie of NSW]. Her sister Flora was m. to Peter McArthur and lived at Ardura in the 1820s. LMD describes Margaret on 24 Jun 1828: "*Margaret Fraser who now lives at Callachilly is the same clever woman she was wont to be. A nurse that she got from Ulva she doubted had made free with some trinkets of value which she had, and having only a suspicion that she had taken them, her husband wished to dissuade her from troubling the woman, but Margaret was not to be put off. She went down to Tighanloan where a Smith of the name of Fraser lives, ordered him to saddle his horse and to carry a pick-lock with him, and mounted behind him off they set for Ulva. Here she got a warrant of search from Col. Macquarie, and with her blacksmith & warrant she sets off for the woman's house whom she took by surprise. She told the woman to deliver the key of her chest, otherwise the smith should open it...the woman protesting her innocence gave up the key and Margaret got every article that she had lost.*" **OPR KLN; GRO/LMD; JC/MIP**

McLean, Margaret (c.1798) w. of **Donald McLean** (q.v.) (c.1793-1897) mercht, she d. Salen Dec. 1892 aged 91, dau. of Rev. Hugh Dewar. and Mary Brisset Campbell. Her s.-in-law John McKenzie, was present at her death. Donald McLean was postmaster at Bunessan.She was b. in Kilmartin.Their ch. were George Duncan, Mary Brisette, Elizabeth, Susan Jane, Hugh, Emily, Maggy.

McLean, Margaret (c.1709-1783) *"Margaret McLean late spouse to Alexander McLean tacksman of Mingary, who departed this life Aug. 1783 aged 74."* **GRV KLN**

McLean,Margaret (c.1801-1864) dau. of Allan McLean crofter & Anne McLean, she m. **Archibald McNiven**, Fanmore and d. 13 Feb. 1864 aged 63.

McLean, Margaret (c. 1809-1892) wid. of **Hector McLean** (q.v.), crofter, she d. aged 83 in 1892 at Dervaig KLM dau. of James McLean farmer and Ann McFadyen. Her s. Alexander McLean gave info at her death. Margaret was bpt. 16 Apr. 1806 at Kilbeg, so her age here is 3 yrs. out.

McLean, Marion (1757-1857) dau. of John McLean, late tacksman Gometra & Mary McPherson w. of **Torquil McQuarrie** whom she m. at Ulva 31 Jan.1792. She lived mainly at Ferininardry in Ulva but d. at Ardmore.

McLean, Marion (c.1785-1857) dau. of Hector McLean servt. & Chirsty McArthur, she m. **Alexander McDougall**; d. 2 May 1857 at Torloisk, aged 72. Perhaps her f. Hector McLean servant, was servant to Maclean of Torloisk, mentioned frequently in **LBP**. This is the only kind of person called 'servant' in this way.

McLean, Marion (c.1782-1861) wid. of **Alexander McLean**, shepherd, she d. Torosay Quinish (sometimes spelt 'Torasa' not to be confused with Torosay parish) aged 79, 1861, of old age. Her parents were Donald McLean crofter & Margaret McLean, M/S McLean.

McLean, Marion (c.1811-1879) d. Assapol 2 Apr. 1879 aged 68, of paralysis, according to evidence of her dau. Christina Rose. Marion, dau. of Donald McLean shepherd & Christina McLucais or McDougall, had m. 1836 **James Rose**. No bpt. for her in **KLF OPR**, but her f. was in 1813 grasskeeper in Ardfenaig.

McLean, Marion (1813-1895) **KLN OPR** gives bpt. as 9 Jun. 1813 at Achnadrish, but GRV at Hamilton, Vic., Australia says she was b. at Achnadrish 2 Jul. 1813. Her parents were Neil & Flora McLeans. She m. **Hector Morrison** (1809-1903) s. of Sergeant Donald Morrison & Jessie Rankin in Drimnacroish. They emig. to Australia in 1854.

McLean, Marion (c.1795-1865) dom. servt. m. to **John McLean** crofter, she d. 1 Feb. 1865 at Penmore KLN aged 70. Her f. was Donald

McEachern crofter and her mo. Mary McDonald.

Maclean, Marion (c.1835-1909) dau. of Alexander McLean ploughman & Christina McEachern, she m. **William Whyte**, ag. lab. at Scour. She d. there 26 Jan 1909 aged 74 of enteritis from info of Alexander Whyte her s.

Maclean, Marianne (1765-1841) of Torloisk, dau. of Lachlan Maclean & Margaret Smith, she was educated & beautiful (figure always noted). She m. Sep. 1790 Gen. **Douglas Clephane** who d. in Grenada 1803. A close friend of Sir Walter Scott, she owed the triumph of m. her dau. Margaret to Lord Compton, later marquis of Northampton, to his diplomacy. The Torloisk estate was later to remain with descendants of the Northampton family, and Lachlan Maclean's handsome, frugal 18th C. Scottish laird's house was disfigured by English Victorian extensions. **JC/MIP**

Maclaine, Mary (c.1740-1831) 'Mally' dau. of Lachlan Maclaine of LB & Katherine McDougall, she m. 1758 as his 2nd w., **Allan McLean** (q.v.) of Drimnin, and was mo. of Donald Maclean WS (q.v.) **JC/MIP** See under Maclaine, Mally.

McLean, Mary (b.1757) dau. of Rev. Alexander McLean (q.v.) min. of Kilninian & Christina McLean, dau. of Donald M. of Torloisk, sister of Hector & Lachlan of T. She m. 16 Nov. 1778, **John Campbell** of Smiddy Green, 2nd s. of Dr Robert Campbell of Smiddy Green, Fife, (who with his w. lived in Virginia until 1779). John Campbell d. 1821. There was 1 s. Robert possibly others. Letters from Mary & John to her bro. John McLean in RHE c.1780 are in **NAS.GD174/1334** & mention her sister Isabel in Torloisk. The letters show John C. intended to go to Virginia after studying English law in London, but refs. in LMD indicate Mary was living in London. *"Waited this day on Mrs John Campbell, Smiddy-Green, 6 Chester Place, Lambeth, near Kensington Cross, on purpose to see her as well as her brother the General...."* LMD Frid. 17 Nov. 1815. Mary is mentioned also in a letter from Hon. Neil McLean 1814 to his s. Alexander as '*a Mrs Campbell in London.*' **AMS/CG. JPM/HCM OPR KLN. GRO/LMD. LBP.**

McLean, Mary (1772-1860) dau. of Neil McLean crofter & Marion McLucash, she d. of the infirmities of old age at 98, in Balligown, 1860, bur. KLN. Her s. John McLean was present at her death. She was bpt. at Balligown 29 Nov. 1772. Her mo. sometimes known as McDougall, another form of McLucash. **CRD** does not give her husb.'s name.

Maclean, Mary (c.1777-1863) m. **Duncan McIntyre**, landed proprietor, Knockvoligan, d. at Knockvoligan aged 86, 23 Oct. 1863 of organic disease of the stomach, in info given by her s. Nicol McIntyre, her parents being Archibald Maclean, farmer & Ann McKichen.

McLean, Mary (c.1778-1862) wid. of **Archibald Colquhoun** ferryman Lochdonhead, dau. of Neil McLean farmer & Mary McPhee, she d aged 84 of old age.

McLean, Mary (d.1834) matron of the Town's Hospital, Glasgow, she was unm., a descendant of John Og McLean in Fishnish. When she d., the executry of her estate was in the hands of Murdoch Maclaine 20th of LB, who had some trouble tracing her relations, but the documentation of the search is in **NAS/GD174/268**, and gives some insights into the genealogy of her family.Among the beneficiaries were the gr.-ch. and gr.-gr.-ch. of her f. [Donald or Daniel McLean, weaver in Glasgow]'s uncle, Neil McLean in Fishnish, some in Mull and some in Greenock. We do not know the dates of these relations, but some are referred to in this work – notably John McLean, carpenter, Greenock; Mary McLean, wid. of Archibald McGilvray, Lochbuy; Janet McLean, wid. of Hugh McLean, workman in Lochbuy; Margaret McLean, wid. of Archibald McDougall, carpenter in Greenock; Catherine McLean, wid. of Neil Carmichael in Ardchrishnish; Charles McLean, tenant in Ardmore; Neil McLean, tenant in Scoball; Ann McLean, w. of Duncan McKechnie in Port Bannatyne [near Rothesay, Island of Bute]; Catherine McLean, w. of John McArthur, tenant in Glenforsa. 10 legatees received £29 4s 2d .

McLean, Mary (c.1781-1861) wid. of **Donald McLean** weaver, dau. of John Currie & Mary McLean, she d. at Craignure, 16 Nov. 1861 aged 80 of 'infirmities of old age', from info of Donald McPhail her nephew. In **CEN TRS 1861** she is at Craignure, 80, pauper, with Sarah Fletcher unm. 64 in 2 rooms. Next door is her nephew Donald McPhail shoemaker 50, with his w. Flora, 33, and their ch. John 5, Neil 3, Donald 3 mos.

McLean, Mary (c.1784-1866) wid., pauper, dau. of Donald McQuarrie, farmer & Janet McLean, she d. 16 Sep. 1866 TBR aged 82 of cancer in armpit. Info from Isabella McKay X dau. occupant, present.

McLaine, Mary (c.1784-1840s) parents unknown, she m. John McCallum from Calgary c.1807, and lived in Ardtun KLF.

McLean, Mary (c.1785-1855) b. Fishnish had lived 70 yrs. in district of Salen and d. 1 Apr.1855 at Fishnish aged 70.Her parents were Donald McPhail farmer & Mary McDonald; she m. **John McPhail**, post messenger, but had no ch., so Archibald McPhail, nephew gave info on her death. A couple with her parents' names were at Ledmore in 1785 and 1787 when their sons Duncan and Malcolm McPhail were bpt. A Donald McPhail was in **ERC/Inhabitants** 1779 at Aros (which could have included Ledmore and Tenga) aged 15, and was the s. of Malcolm McPhail aged 50.

McLean,Mary (c.1789-1860), crofter's wid., she d. of the infirmities of old age at Penmore 26 Aug. 1860 aged 71, dau. of John McLean crofter & Mary McDonald.

McLean, Mary (c.1789-1875) wid. of **Donald McLean**, late mercht. Tobermory, she d. 17 Nov. 1875 at Shore Street TBR aged 86. Her f. was Donald McPhee and her mo. Mary McLean.

McLean, Mary (18th C.) m. **Archibald McGilvray** in LB. A dau. of Hector McLean in Glenbyre & Flora McLean, gr.-dau. of Neil McLean in Fishnish, she was one of the beneficiaries of the Will of Miss Mary McLean (q.v.), matron of the Town's Hospital, Glasgow, who d. 1834.

McLean, Mary (c.1790-1882) wid. of **Allan Maclean**, farmer, she d. 27 Mar. 1882 at 9am at Rockcliff, TBR aged 100, dau. of Lachlan McLean, tacksman & Mary McLean, M/S McGilvray, both dec. of an unknown illness, and with no med. att. from the info of her nephew John McCallum, Solicitor. **Note:** When her husband Allan d. at Creich on 10 Feb.1857, they were living in Creich/Catchean area. She went to Tobermory where she lived with her McCallum nephews and nieces, but John McCallum has made a mistake about her mo.'s M/S. Her mo. was in fact Mary McLean of Torrans. Her husb. Allan Maclean (c.1785-1857) was in Van Diemen's Land (Tasmania) < their marr., but it is not known why. This was the dau. of Lachlan Ban McLean (q.v.), Bunessan & Mary McLean M/S. McLean **not** McGillivray. Her gr.mo. was a McGillivray.

McLean, Mary (c.1798-1882) m. **Charles McLean**, crofter; she d. aged 84, 9 Jan. 1882, at

Kinloch, dau. of John McInnes, crofter & Sarah McLean; info from Charles McLean, husb.

Maclaine, Mary (1800-1880) dau. of Murdoch Maclaine 19th of LB & Jane Campbell, she m. John Gregorson of Ardtornish 12 Sep. 1820. See **JC/MIP**. She d. aged 80 at Castle Street, Edinburgh 11 August 1880, us. res. Upper Norwood, London. Her med. att. was Joseph Bell, the prototype of Sherlock Holmes. A sweet personality, she was adored by LMD. **JC/MIP**

McLean, Mary (c.1801-1876) m. to **Alexander McLean**, farmer, dau. of Samuel McLachlan farmer & Ann McLean, she d. at Achnadrish KLN on 12 May 1876 aged 75, of old age. Info from her nephew, Kenneth McDonald.

McLean, Mary (c.1809-1886) d. wid. of **Neil McCallum** at Creich 24 Jul. 1886 aged 77 of valvular disease of the heart cert.by Alexander MacKechnie, info from her s. Lachlan McCallum. Her f. was Hector McLean, shoemaker & crofter, her mo. Marion McKinnon. Her f. must have d. between 1814 and 1826, as her mo. Marion m. Lachlan McKinnon in Jan. 1826.

McLean, Mary (c.1810-1860) dau. of John McPhail & Marion McDougall; m. **Charles McLean**; d. 31 Oct. 1860 at Ledirkle aged 50; bur. Pennygown. CRD signed by her husb. Charles McLean. **CRD TRS** In **CEN TRS 1851** at Garmony, following Ledirkle, there is a Charles McLean aged 55, cotton weaver, b. Gribun, with Mary, w. 39 b. TRS, Ann, dau. 3 & Marion McLean, relation, wid., 83 b. Gribun. In 1861 Charles McLaine [sic] is wid. 65, wool weaver, with dau. Anne 13.

McLean, Mary (c.1810-1860) dau. of Alexander McDougall weaver & Margaret Morrison, she was a crofter's w. who d. 9 Oct. 1860 at Penmore aged 50.

McLean, Mary Ann (1811-1894) wid. of **Colin Campbell**, landed proprietor, she d. at Ardfenaig aged 83 in 1894. She was bpt. 21 Jan. 1811, dau. of Hector McLean (q.v.) of Mingary & Helen Campbell, who had had 7 boys in succession in **KLN OPR** followed by 4 girls in a row. She came from sound tacksman stock, being a gr.dau. of Anne Maclean of Torloisk and of Mr Donald Campbell, Chamberlain of Tiree.

McLean, Mary (b.1813) dau. of Donald McLean & Flora McFee, she was bpt. at Iona in 1813, m. on 10 Feb. 1842, **Duncan Maclean** from the Parish of Ross. Two daus. were reg. on 10 Jan.

1844 – Ann, b. 6 Nov. 1842, and Effy b. 6 Dec. 1843. In **CEN KLF 1851** she is in Scoor, a wid., aged only 35 making a living by knitting with another ch., Neil, 5. She is identified by the presence of her mo. 'Flora McFee' (enumerators forgot to write marr. names). Flora was 76 and the census tells us she was b. at Knocknafenaig, so that she was probably one of the daus. of the 2 McDiffies there in **ERC/Inhabitants 1779**. McDiffie or McDuffie is a variant of McFee or McPhie. Mary was still at Scour in 1861, with Effy 17 and Neil 15.

McLaine, Mary (<1815) d. 19 Feb. 1856 at Torlochan SLN dau. of Lachlan McLaine shepherd & Sarah McGillivray. She had no med. att., and was bur. at Knock SLN. Her bro. Charles McLaine, Rohill, Glenforsa gave info. This Charles MacLean (nb. different spellings) was 40 and a shepherd in **CEN SLN 1851** Rohill, with Margaret 43 b. Kilbrandon; with ch. 'scholars'- Margaret 14, John 11, Dugal 9, Ann 7, Mary 5, Catherine 3 – all b. SLN.

McLean, Mary (c.1820-1892) dau. of Alexander McLean crofter & Catherine Kennedy, wid. of **Duncan McLean**, crofter, she d. 10 Feb. 1892 at Dervaig aged 72 of influenza, her s. Hector Maclean present.

McLean, Mary (c.1825-1905) dau. of John McInnes farmer & Ann McLean; m. to **Archibald McLean**, farmer, she d. at Ballygown 25 Jan. 1905 aged 80 of 'old age'. Her s. Malcolm McLean present.

McLean, Muddock (fl.1600-1700) a Mull witch whose imprecations fell on enemies of the Macleans. As she had sworn to keep the earls of Argyll from the island, the great storm of 1675 which drove back the Campbell ships was believed to be her doing. Mull witches, Na Doideagan, were real people with the gift of prophecy, who were midwives, physicians, and seers. Even in the 20th C. there were a number of witches in Mull, whose deeds were regarded as being supernatural, who lived alone, many unm. or widowed older women, but it is now difficult to ascertain their exact names. Several were Macleans, like the one who was instrumental in sinking a Spanish Armada ship in 1588. **JPM/HCM**

Maclaine, Murdoch (1730-1804) linen mercht. in Edinburgh, s. of Lachlan M. of Knockroy & Flora McQuarrie, he m. (1) Anne Learmonth who d.1780 without issue, succeeded to estate of

Lochbuy after dramatic murder of his cousin Archy in 1784, m. (2) 1786 Jane Campbell of Airds by whom he had Jane 1787, Margaret 1789, Elizabeth 1790, Murdoch (his successor) 1791, John 1792, Catherine 1793, Phoebe 1795, Flora 1796, Harriet 1798, Mary 1800, Jane Jarvis 1802. His story told in detail in **JC/MIP**

Maclaine, Murdoch (1774-1822) s. of Farquhar Maclaine (q.v. 'honest Farquhar') & Betty Macquarie, he was bpt. 18 Sep. 1774 at Oskamull. Joined army c.1793 when there was some question of his leaving [letter, 4 July 1793, CM to MM **GD174/1484/6**] Later, "*my nephew Murdoch has been recommended to the War Office at Dublin*" 1795 [**GD174/1484/51**] "*Murdoch made a Lieutenant – Lachlan will be astonished*" **GD174/1484/60** "*I have a long letter from Murdoch from Gibraltar – well & hearty- but lives expensively…*" **GD174/1484/63**. In 1813, "*I was happy to hear of Capt. Murdoch's arrival – his poor parents will be much gratified to see him.*" [Jane Campbell, w. of MM to her s. MM2 GD174/1626/1] 2nd Mar. 1814, "*Capt. Murdoch Maclaine 42nd is in Edinburgh…*" IBID. /6] This time in Edinburgh coincides with date of conception of Jean 'McLean' his dau. b. Edinburgh to Hannah Roebuck, but no marr. found. See entry for McLean, Jean (c.1815-1878). Murdoch's military promotion was Lieut. 37th Regt. 1796; Capt. 7th W. India Regt. 1804; Capt. 42nd Regt. (Royal Highland) 16 Jun.1808; Brevet Major 4 Jun. 1814; left Army 1814. [Military info from RW Munro]. **OPR KLN. LBP. GRO/LMD**

McLean, Murdoch (18th C.) weaver in Tiroran, m. **Catherine McNeill**. See McLean, Charles (c.1799-1887) his s.

Maclaine, Murdoch (1791-1844) 20th of LB, s. of Murdoch 19th & Jane Campbell, m. 1813 **Christina McLean**, dau. of Donald McLean WS (q.v.) & Lillias Grant. They had 12 ch. see **JC/MIP** His heir Murdoch (1814-1850) was a bitter disappointment, and took his f. to court over the question of the entail. With Murdoch 20th's death came the demise of many LB traditions, like affiliation to the C. of S.and practical use of Gaelic. His main problems were his heir, harsh economic conditions and escalating debt, which he kept at bay with hard drinking and his favourite sport of stag-shooting. His foible was a notion that he was Chief of the clan Maclean.

McLean, Murdoch (1795-1882) also 'Maclaine', pauper, formerly farm servant, wid. of **Mary**

Colquhoun, s. of Charles McLean (q.v.) & Cirsty Black, he d. 17 Aug. 1882, at Balimeanach TRS aged 84 (actually 87?) of 'climacteric decay' from info of Alexander McDougall, Insp. of Poor. **CRD TRS 1882**. He was in **CEN TRS 1881** as a wid. 84 with sister Catherine wid. of a soldier, 79 & niece Mary McLean 38. See Maclaine, Donald (c.1794-1855) his bro. There were 2 Murdoch 'Maclaines' of similar ages brought up in Ledirkle, near Fishnish.

McLean, Murdoch (1806) bpt. 22 May 1806 s. of Donald & Janet McLeans Crogan KLS; m. **Janet Rankin**, Drimnatyne 8 Dec. 1842. Their dau. Anne b. 5 Nov. 1845.

McLean, Murdoch (c.1863-1865) s. of Murdoch McLean blacksmith & Isabella McLean, M/S Nairne, he d. in Edinburgh 1865 aged 18 mos.

Maclaine, Murdoch Gillean (1845-1909) of LB, s. of Donald Maclaine (q.v.) of LB & Emilie Guillaumine Vincent, he m. **Catherine Marianne Schwabe**; d. 5 Apr. 1909 at 10.45pm at 'Lochbuie Castle, Isle of Mull', KLS – the only death recorded there in 1909, aged 63 of kidney disease as related by Capt. Edwyn S. Dawes his s.-in-law, Greenford Place, Harrow, England [2nd husb. of Kathleen Maclaine]. **CRD KLS. CEN TRS 1881** has the family of LB at Moy on census day: Murdoch Gillean McLaine 35 b. Java; Katharine Marianna McLaine 30 b. Manchester; Kathleen Julia McLaine 10, Mabel Emilia 8, Edith Jane 4, Kenneth Douglas Lorne McLaine (q.v.) a baby of 14 mo., all b. in London. 7 servants were in residence. At this time Lochbuie House was usually let, and the enumerator was lucky to catch the family in Scotland. The names Kathleen, Mabel & Edith are perpetuated in 3 cottages at LB today.

McLaine, Neil (<1720?-1767) wright & joiner in Ulva m. to **Christian McQuarrie**. His executry papers are in **GRO/Glouc**. with bills from Dr McQuary Ormaig for attendance, from ferryman Angus McQuarrie & Angus McKinnon tailor in Corkamull.

McLean, Neil (<1750) f. of Mary McLean (1772-1860) husb. of **Marion McLucaish or McDougall**. See Flora McLean (c.1775-1870) his dau. He lived at Lagganulva when he m. Mairon 19 Dec. 1769. Bpts. at Balligown, Fanmore & Torloisk: Mary 1772, Donald 1775, John 1778, Flora 1780.

McLean, Neil (<1755) m. **Mary McPhie,**

according to **CRD** of Mary Colquhoun (c.1778-1862), his dau.

McLean, Neil (<1760) "Neil Piper" bagpiper to Murdoch Maclaine of Lochbuy, he went to America with MM in 1782, when he wrote to his f. in Mull by Gillean Maclaine to say he had 1 girl, and 1 boy called Hector, and a cousin John Ogilby settled 10 mls. from New York. In 1783 he intended to return to Mull from 84th Regt. but wrote from Halifax, NS 1794 to MM "*I now have 5 promising Boys & a Girl... my eldest Boy Hector is with your old acquaintance Peter McNab, shoemaker, and my second son John is with Messrs. Kerstrey, Tallow Chandlers...*" **NAS GD174/1348, 1349. GD174/1501.**

McLean, Neil (b.c.1760) m. **Flora McKinnon** and was a shepherd at Torrans.

McLean, Neil (<1773) m. 29 July 1795 **Christina McInnes** Balligown. Bpts were Margaret 1795, Archibald 1800, n.k. 1802, Hector 1804, Flora 1807, Mary 1810, Marion 1813. Like many in Balligown, which prob. had a clearance at this time, they vanish > 1814.

McLean, Neil (<1775) m. **Catherine McInnes**. She d. 10 Jan.1868 aged 99 at Ardalanish KLF wid. of Neil McLean. Her f. was Donald McInnes; her mo. Catherine McInnes M/S McInnes. Her s. Hector McLean 74 d. 3 wks. later at Ardalanish. John McLean, who could not write his name, s. of Neil & Catherine, gave info at his mo.'s & bro.'s deaths.

McLean, Neil (<1785) m. **Flora McLean** 'publickly' [suggesting a celebration] both in Sorne, KLN, 19 Mar.1805; their ch. bpt. at Sorne were Christina (q.v.)1806, Hector 1808, John 1812, Marion 1813, Hugh 1817, John 1819, Anne 1822. Other ch. may be unrecorded because of GK. No obvious remnant appears in **CEN 1841, 1851** in Sorne area, but the survival of Christina into old age shows they did not all leave Mull. Neil's details are not incompatible with those of Neil McLean immediately below, and the fluctuation of ages in records makes the theory that they were the same admissable.

McLean, Neil (c.1779-1858)s. of John McLean & Janet McLean M/S McLean, he m. <1812, but his w.'s name has not been discovered, as he was probably already a wid. in 1841 census at Kilmore, but enumerated as wid. in 1851 at Aintuim, KLN. He is known to have had a s. Hector who predeceased him, c. mid 1840s, aged

about 36. Neil was the subject of a letter sent by the factor of the Coll estates in 1849, Donald Campbell to Hugh Maclean of Coll, saying that he had had to warn Neil, although he did not remove him. Most of his possession was given to a neighbour, Allan McDonald. "*Neil McLean is not able to pay his arrears, and he is thankful and grateful for the arrangement I have made to keep him in part of his possession at least for this year*." As Neil d. at Aintuim, 14 Jan. 1858, mercy was shown. His s. Hector had left a wid., Janet and a young s., Donald McLean, b.c.1842, and probably other ch. **CRD KLN. CEN KLN 1841, 1851. DC/LB Mull Museum** See entry for Neil McLean immediately above.

McLean, Neil (c.1780) small farmer in various places in Ross of Mull he m. **Flora McFarlan** in 1811 when he was in Suie and she in Ardtun. 10 ch. were bpt. – Ann 1812; Margaret 1814; Mary 1817; Archibald 1819; Duncan 1821; Catherine 1824; Cirsty 1826; Marion 1829, Cirsty in 1831 and another Cirsty in 1837. In **CEN KLF 1851** the family is in Ardalanish. The death of his wid. Flora in 1880 at Lee, giving her age as 88 makes her 19 on marr., and makes it possible to have this spread of births. This couple had a McLachlan gr.-ch. b. in Paisley (Neil, b.c.1845) indicating a drift to the Scottish lowlands of their ch.

McLean, Neil (c.1784-1876) s. of Hector McLean farmer & Christian McArthur, wid. of **Catherine Campbell**, he d. at Fanmore KLN 1876 aged 92 of old age, his bro. John McLean present. Parents Hector & Christian were m. 6 Jan. 1778, Hector from KLF. They may be the same as H. McLean 34, & w. in Knocknafenaig in **ERC/Inhabitants** 1779, as their 1st 4 ch., John, Archibald, Marion & Flora were recorded in **KLN OPR** as being bpt. in KLF. But no Neil! By 1795 they were in Raodle.

McLean, Neil (b. c.1790) in Crogan, TRS, he was m. to **Catherine Cameron** 27 Jan. 1814. Their ch. were Isabel 1815; Donald 1817; John 1819; John 1821; Lachlan 1823; Neil 1824; Cirsty 1827 and Robert 1829.

McLean, Neil (<1782) tenant in Scobull KLF s. of Duncan McLean & Mary McLaine, gr.s. of Neil McLean in Fishnish, he is one of the beneficiaries in the executry of the Will of Miss Mary McLean (q.v. – d.1834), his cousin, matron of the Town's Hospital, Glasgow. He can almost certainly be identified with Neil McLaine in **CEN KLF 1841** at 'Scoble' aged 55 farmer, with Flora 40, John 20, Donald 10, Hector 8, Mary 6. His w.

was **Flora McLean**. He had been tenant in Tapul from <1825, sons Duncan, Donald & Hector being bpt. there in 1825, 1830 and 1832.

McLean, Neil (c.1792) weaver in Ardtun, Ross of Mull, he m. Bland McEachern in Bunessan KLF 9 Feb. 1813, and hovered between 3 places of abode, Bunessan, Torranuachdrach and Ardtun before settling in Ardalanish c.1828. There were 7 known ch., Hector 1813; Allan 1816; Isabella 1818; Mary 1821; Charles 1823; Lachlan 1826 and Duncan 1829. He & Bland were both reported to be 45 in **CEN KLF 1841** at Ardalanish.

McLean, Rev. Neil (1797-1864) gr.s. of John McLean (b.1729) tenant in Acharn, s. of Charles McLean (q.v.) (b.1767) who left Mull to live in MRV, & Euphemia Campbell;he was only known surviving s. among 4 sisters, and was sent to be educated in Iona by his scholarly uncle Allan McLean (q.v.) (c.1760-1853). Destined for the ministry, he had to fill in time by tutoring, and taught ch. of Charles Macquarie (later proprietor of Ulva) until his patron secured him Ulva QS parish in 1828. He is highly spoken of in **GRO LMD** both as preacher and as conversationalist. He m. in 1840, **Clementina Clark**, sister of F.W. Clark of Ulva, and had 7 ch. - Agnes Wright 1842-1860; Clementina Anderson 1843-1878; Charles 1845-1897; Isabella Campbell b.1846;Neil 1848-1878; Francis William Clark 1849-1885; John Anderson 1853-1912. **JC/MIP**

McLean, Neil (c.1798-1878) s. of Neil McLean weaver & Marion McDonald, he was pensioner of Bengal Horse Artillery m. to **Flora Campbell**, and d. at Kinloch KLF 1878 aged 80. He was in **CEN KLF 1851** Kinloch in household of Malcolm Campbell his f.-in-law 49 with Flora 26, and Neil was then 51. In 1861 he was still at Kinloch aged 62 with Flora 36, Donald 15, Marion 10 scholar, Allan 7 scholar, in the house immediately behind Malcolm Campbell & Marion McMillan, his in-laws. In 1871 there is Malcolm 6, and Marion McMillan has become a wid. "Sarah Campbell" and is 68. There is a niece Mary Kirkwood 12, scholar, living with them.

McLean, Neil (1809-1883) fisherman m. to **Catherine McLean**, he d. 19 April 1883 Argyll Terr., TBR of cardiac failure, aged 74. He was bpt. 21 Mar. 1809 in Tobermory, s. of Angus McLean lab. & Catherine McPherson. Info from his s. Donald McLean.

McLean, Neil (c.1813) fisherman b. TBR, he m. **Catherine Buchanan** (b. 7 Mar. 1824 at Mingary)

Nov. 1852 at Kilmore. 5 sons and 1 dau. were b. at Ardow and Cragaig – John c.1853, Bell 1856, Donald c.1858, Duncan c.1860, Lizzie 1862, Alexander, Angus. Catherine Buchanan's parents prob. John Buchanan & Ann Livingston.

Maclean, Neil [Whiteside] (1820-1909) s. of Dr Allan Maclean (q.v.) the 'red-haired doctor' & Flora Maclaine (q.v.) of LB,the name Whiteside was adopted later, probably in gratitude for the kindness of his step-f., Dr Wm. Whiteside (1793-1862) and was passed down to some of his descendants. He was b. at 'dear Rossal' nr. L. Scridain in Mull, and on LB estate, but left after his f.'s death in 1827 with his mo., bros. and sisters to live in Ayr. His mo., listing her ch.'s potential careers in 1828, thought Neil likely to become a shepherd. From 1830-32, Neil was tutored at LB with his cousin Allan, but to what use he put this is not known. He m. 2 Oct. 1852 at Geelong, Victoria, Australia, **Isabella (or Sibella) McKinnon** (1827-1911) dau. of Hector McKinnon of Derriguaig in Mull & Catherine McLean (q.v.)Their 8 sons, b. in Australia, bear all the names of the parents' distinguished Mull ancestry: Allan Murdoch Whiteside Maclean 1853; Joseph William Henry Maclean 1855; Archibald Lachlan McKinnon Maclean 1855; Donald Alexander Neil Maclean 1859; Charles Hector Maclean 1861; Hugh John McKinnon Maclean 1864; Philip William Whiteside Maclean 1867; John Samuel Maclean 1870. Neil Whiteside Maclean was gr.s. to Murdoch Maclaine 19th of LB (who d. in 1804) & Jane Campbell of Airds (who d. when he was 4). Some descendants are known to be in W. Australia and Victoria today. **NAS GD174/1634JC/MIP**

McLean, Neil (c.1823) shepherd b. Balligown, he m. 1846, Ulva Parish, **Marion McMillan** b.c.1822. From 1855 birth of their dau. Catherine at hamlet of Kilninian, Marion's 4th ch., there were then 2 other girls & 1 boy living. In **CEN KLN 1861** Neil is 39, Sara Macmillan 39, Angus 13, Ann 11, Flora 9, Catherine 5, Allan 3 & Archibald 7. The last is a gr.s.

McLean, Neil (c.1826?) lab. aged 29 at Tostary KLN when his s. Lachlan was b. 20 Oct. 1855 thus giving an unusually extended CRB. Neil was b. Ardow and m. 1849 Ulva Parish, **Marion Robertson** (33 in 1855 giving birth to her 3rd ch.) who was b. at Oskamull. In **CEN KLN 1861** he is 35, with Marion 37, Charles 10, Malcolm 7, Lachlan 5, Allan 3 mos. A mo.-in-law, wid., 60, called Chirsty McMillan makes for confusion with Neil McLean above, especially since a large family of Robertsons at Oskamull were ch. of William Robertson & Sarah McKinnon.

McLean, Neil (c.1832) shepherd 29 at Balligown in **CEN KLN 1861** with w. **Mary McDougall** 36, dau. Sara 5, dau. Margaret 3 & dau. Flora 1. His bpt. is lost in GK, so his details have to be reconstructed.

McLean, Neil (1840-1866) s. of John McLaine farmer & Ann Cameron, he was a schoolmaster in Kinloch who d. of laryngitis aged 25 in 1866.

Maclean, Norman (1877-1946) of Pennycross, 3rd s. of Archibald John Maclean of PX & Carsaig, whose estate was sold in 1888, after many battles to retain it in the family, not least on the part of Norman's mo., Isabelle Alexandrina Simon, who d. at Carsaig in Feb. 1886, shortly after giving birth to her 4th dau. The Macleans of PX lived at Tiroran after their tribulations. At this time the McVean family were tenants of Killiemore House. Iona McVean remembered Norman in her *Memories of Mull*. Speaking of the reels danced at balls in the last quarter of the 19th C. she wrote :"*I have a vivid recollection of Norman McLean of Pennycross at one of those dances (tall, dashing, like all the Pennycrosses!) dancing a Polka to the tune of 'See me dance the Polka' with our very pretty little dairymaid, and singing at the pitch of his voice, 'My bonny wee Mary-Ann, you're the bonniest lass in the barn.' This same Norman one day in our dining room asked our mother who the lovely girl was in the petticoat above the sofa. My mother told him it was a portrait of herself before she was married. Norman knelt down beside her and put his arms round her waist and kissed her, saying, 'Oh, why wasn't I a laddie then!'*" He m. in 1900 **Hylda FM Green**.

McLean, Patrick (bpt.1824) s. of Charles McLean (q.v.) the Penmore boatman & Mary McLucaish, also from Penmore KLN, he was 26 in **CEN KLN 1851**, living with bro. Archibald 23, wid. mo. Mary 54 and 2 nephews, Hugh (8) & Hector (6) McLean. In **CEN KLN 1861** he had Sheeblie McKinnon 15, niece and Lachlan McKinnon 12 nephew with him at Penmore. In 1871 he was 44, having m. **Flora McMaster** in 1862, and with his own ch., Ann 8, Hector 4, Charles 1. No increase in ch. in **CEN KLN 1881** is due to his w. being 13 years older. Known as Peter in censuses, Peter & Patrick being

interchangeable names.

McLean, Peggy (c. 1785-1860) wid. of Duncan McLean late of Ardmore she d. 5 Sep.1860 at Crag-na-spiure TBR, aged 75. Her parents were Hugh McLean, miller & crofter, Penmore KLN & Mary Campbell. ('Cragnaspure' in **CEN KLN 1871** follows Penalbanach (1 house) and Ardmore (1 house) and is lived in by a McLean family – John McLean, carpenter 40, b.KLN and his w. Margaret, 30 b. Kilchoan ARD, with 3 ch., his unm. bro.Malcolm McLean, 56, weaver. The 2nd of the 3 houses at Crag-na-spure has another McLean family, Hugh, 50, unm., farmer and crofter b. Kilninian with 2 sisters and 1 bro. + McKinnon nephews & nieces.

McLean, Peter (1826-1893) proprietor of Gometra, s. of Hector McLean (q.v.) & Flora McArthur, remained a bachelor, succeeding to Gometra on the death of his bros. Donald McLean (q.v.) in 1871, then John (q.v.), 17 Feb. 1893; sole owner of the island for 3mos. when he d. Kingharair KLN of dyspepsia, his nephew Donald McLachlan being present at his death.

McLean, Peter (bpt. 1824) <u>see</u> McLean, Patrick (bpt.1824) m. to Flora McMaster.

McLean, Peter (1859-1940) MD.JP. <u>see</u> GRV for Catherine McDonald his mo. who d.1886. He was in **CEN KLN 1881** at Dervaig aged 22, med. stud., his f. Hector McLean farmer and his bro. John 24 postmaster & mercht. <u>See</u> McLean, Hector (1813-1896) for more about family.

Maclean, Roderick (c.1849-1923) fisherman wid. of **Emma Campbell**, d. 5 Aug. 1923 at 55 Main Street TBR, aged 74 of angina, s. of Neil Maclean carpenter & Margaret Campbell according to his s. Neil.

McLean, Sarah (1852-1944) dau. of George McLean (q.v.) by his 2nd w. Sarah McNeill. She m. **Donald McLean** in Langamull. **GRV KLN** says, "*In loving memory of Sarah McLean who died at Tobermory 6 Feb. 1944 in her 93rd year, wife of the late Donald McLean, Langamull, and of her mother Sarah McNeill who died at Kilninian 27 March 1889 in her 74th year, wife of the late George McLean, Burg.*" Donald d. 2 Dec. 1910 in his 78th year, s. of Charles McLean (q.v.) & Mary Livingston.

Maclean, Sibella (c.1753 ?) dau. of Sir Allan Maclean (q.v.) & Una Maclean of Coll, m. 1779 **John Maclean** of Inverscadale and was only ch. of Sir Allan to have ch. – 1s. unm. & 1 dau., Mary

Ann, who m. Dr Mackenzie Grieve, from whom any claimants of relationship must descend. <u>See</u> Maclean, John (<1740).

Maclean, Sibella (1804-1878) dau. of Donald McLean WS, she m. **Alexander Crawford** (1809-1856) a Mull landowner. Their ch. were Lillias 1832-1910, Sibella 1834-1897, Donald 1837-1919, Christian 1839-1842 and Adelaide 1841-1878.

McLean, Susan (1808-1883) dau. of Dugald McLean, tacksman of Ardfenaig & Susan Macleod, m. 1837 Rev. Donald McVean (1808-1880); ch. Colin Alexander (1838-1912), Helen Susan 1839, Anne Catherine 1840, Susan Isabella 1842, Mary Helen 1843, Dugald Hector 1845, Isabella Merriman 1846, Archibald Arthur 1848. Her husb. joined FC in Disruption 1843, and was min. of Iona FC till 1875. She d. Cawdor Place, Oban 10 Nov.1883 aged 75.

McLean, Susanna (<1730) housekeeper to John Mackinnon, Heir of Provision to attainted Mackinnon of Mackinnon at Mishnish, accused of being his mistress by Presb. of Mull in 1751, removed from his house at Erray KLN, but went only a mile to Portmore. She was reprimanded, stripped of her possessions and sent from Mull.

McLean, Thomas (b.1820) an unusual Christian name for Mull Macleans, this Thomas was prob. the s. of Neil McLean in Garmony & Catherine McInnes. He was a shepherd 40 in Mingary in **CEN KLN 1861** with a w. Marion 41 and ch. Mary 13, Duncan11, Donald 9, Catherine 5, all 'scholars'. There were also 2 Thomas McLeans, 15 & 13 in **CEN KLF 1841** at Tirergain.

Maclean, Una (d.1760) dau. of Hector Maclean of Coll and his 1st w. Janet Campbell of Lochnell, carefully educated like most of her family, she m. Sir Allan Maclean (q.v.) about the time of his accession to the title, and prob. lived mainly in the shadow of her mo.-in-law, Isabel Maclean of Ardgour, when Sir Allan was abroad in the army. Her greatest grief the death of her small s. Lauchlan, who might have inherited title of Duart and changed history of Mull. 3 daus, Maria, Sibilla (q.v.) and Anne remained to comfort Sir Allan's widowhood, for Una d. in her thirties, and the title, after her husb.'s death, reverted to a Maclean cousin overseas.